THE
SECOND
IMPEACHMENT
REPORT

THE

SECOND

IMPEACHMENT

REPORT

*Materials in Support of H. Res. 24, Impeaching Donald John Trump,
President of the United States, for High Crimes and Misdemeanors*

Report by the Majority Staff of the House Committee on the Judiciary

FOREWORD BY

MICHAEL COHEN

HOT BOOKS
an imprint of Skyhorse Publishing, Inc.
New York, NY

Copyright © 2021 by Hot Books, an imprint of Skyhorse Publishing
Foreword © 2021 by Michael Cohen

Hot Books may be purchased in bulk at special discounts for sales promotion, corporate gifts, fund-raising, or educational purposes. Special editions can also be created to specifications. For details, contact the Special Sales Department, Skyhorse Publishing, 307 West 36th Street, 11th Floor, New York, NY 10018 or info@skyhorsepublishing.com.

Hot Books® and Skyhorse Publishing® are registered trademarks of Skyhorse Publishing, Inc.®, a Delaware corporation.

Visit our website at www.skyhorsepublishing.com.

10 9 8 7 6 5 4 3 2 1

Library of Congress Cataloging-in-Publication Data is available on file.

Cover design by Brian Peterson

Print ISBN: 978-1-5107-6730-0
Ebook ISBN: 978-1-5107-6731-7

Printed in the United States of America

THE

SECOND

IMPEACHMENT

REPORT

FOREWORD

On January 6, 2021, I watched in disbelief and terror as a group of protestors descended on the Capitol in a shocking act of insurrection against our republic. This wasn't the kind of event that happens in America, or so we thought. These protestors stormed our nation's Capitol, destroyed public property, and terrorized government officials who were forced to evacuate their chambers and go into hiding. In the end, five people, including a law enforcement officer, were dead. Images of the QAnon Shaman, the Confederate flag, and men scaling the walls around the Capitol building will be burned indelibly into the memories of millions who witnessed these events or watched them unfold on television or on social media. Unified in their support for President Donald J. Trump, these protestors had one goal in mind: to stop the electoral count and prevent Joe Biden from taking office.

What is probably the most important aspect of this entire scenario is that these protestors were not rogue anarchists creating chaos for the hell of it. These people were acting on orders. The orders came directly from the president who has repeatedly refused to concede the election. They came from a president who threatened his vice president and tried to force him to act against the laws of our constitution. They came from a president who has told white supremacists, fascists, and Nazis to "stand back, stand by," and wait for his signal. He delivered this signal in a speech outside the Capitol on the now infamous day of January 6, 2021. In this speech Trump proclaimed, "We will never concede," and "You'll never take back our country with weakness. You have to show strength, and you have to be strong." The call to "take back" America by force emboldened thousands of rioters to attempt a coup. Trump's incendiary remarks about election fraud and his refusal to acknowledge the legitimacy of Biden's victory directly resulted in this day of sedition—and many saw it coming. For weeks leading up to the horrific events in Washington, DC, he and his supporters had been telling us that this would be a day of reckoning. And so it was.

As the live impeachment coverage plays continuously, I think back to my testimony before the U.S. House of Representatives Committee on Oversight and Reform. I closed my testimony to Congress with the following words: "My loyalty to Mr. Trump has cost me everything: my family's happiness, friendships, my law license, my company, my livelihood, my honor, my reputation, and soon, my freedom. And I will not sit back, say nothing, and allow him to do the same to the country . . . Indeed, given my experience working for Mr. Trump, I fear that if he loses the election in 2020 that there will never be a peaceful transition of power . . ." It gives me no satisfaction to know that I was indeed correct almost two years ago.

Since January 6, the country—and the world—has been glued to television, computer, and cell phone screens, fearful of what might happen next. The House of Representatives, led by Nancy Pelosi, took swift and decisive action. Joined by ten

Republicans, they made Donald Trump the first president in United States history to be impeached twice. Some have argued this action wasn't warranted or worth it, given that Mr. Trump had only days left in office.

But increasingly, a large group of lawmakers and millions of Americans believed that he could be a danger to the republic and to our national security and that he must be held accountable for inciting an insurrection.

Others have said that impeaching Donald Trump would divide the country at a time when we need to heal. I believe that if we did nothing, those responsible for the reprehensible actions of January 6, 2021, would feel emboldened to cause even more damage. By impeaching Donald J. Trump a second time, we made it nearly impossible for him to seek federal office again. And, if he's convicted after a trial by the Senate, he cannot legally run for president again, and he would not be entitled to any of the benefits former presidents usually receive. Most importantly, his impeachment has sent a message to future office holders that we are a nation of laws and that our elected officials have pledged allegiance to the Constitution, not to an individual. In order for this country to truly heal, Trumpism must be purged and eradicated. America is built on a foundation of tolerance, freedom, and free and fair elections. We must return to these values.

Over the last few years, I have had to pay the price and repent for my misdeeds as Mr. Trump's attorney. However, paying off a porn star pales in comparison to the actions taken by Trump's supporters on January 6, 2021. Rudy Giuliani warmed up the crowd awaiting Trump's speech on January 6 by proclaiming

"Let's have trial by combat." It is clear that the Trump administration has gone too far this time. I will say it once again—they must be held accountable.

What follows in these pages is a cogent and compelling argument for why the 45th President of the United States of America had to be impeached again and should be convicted by the Senate. We should never have to call Donald Trump "Mr. President" again after January 20, 2021.

Michael Cohen

MATERIALS IN SUPPORT OF H. RES. 24, IMPEACHING DONALD JOHN TRUMP, PRESIDENT OF THE UNITED STATES, FOR HIGH CRIMES AND MISDEMEANORS

———

REPORT BY THE MAJORITY STAFF OF THE HOUSE COMMITTEE ON THE JUDICIARY

———

Prepared for Chairman Jerrold Nadler

UNITED STATES
JANUARY 2021

Majority Staff

Amy Rutkin, Chief of Staff
Perry Apelbaum, Staff Director and Chief Counsel
John Doty, Senior Advisor
Aaron Hiller, Deputy Chief Counsel
David Greengrass, Senior Counsel
John Williams, Parliamentarian and Senior Counsel
Shadawn Reddick-Smith, Communications Director
Moh Sharma, Director of Member Services and Outreach & Policy Advisor
Arya Hariharan, Deputy Chief Oversight Counsel
James Park, Chief Counsel of Constitution Subcommittee
Sarah Istel, Counsel
Matthew Morgan, Counsel
Madeline Strasser, Chief Clerk
William S. Emmons, Legislative Aide
Priyanka Mara, Legislative Aide
Anthony Valdez, Legislative Aide
Jessica Presley, Director of Digital Strategy
Kayla Hamedi, Deputy Press Secretary

MATERIALS IN SUPPORT OF H. RES. 24, IMPEACHING DONALD JOHN TRUMP, PRESIDENT OF THE UNITED STATES, FOR HIGH CRIMES AND MISDEMEANORS

HOUSE JUDICIARY COMMITTEE
MAJORITY STAFF REPORT

JANUARY 12, 2021

INTRODUCTION

The Constitution grants the House of Representatives the "sole Power of Impeachment," not merely as a safeguard for the nation between elections, but also in cases where the removal of the President is urgent and necessary to preserve the security of the constitutional order. The House must invoke this power now to impeach President Trump for inciting an insurrection on January 6, 2021. President Trump engaged in high Crimes and Misdemeanors when he urged his supporters to storm the United States Capitol Building and then failed to stop the ensuing violence. His actions marked the culmination of an extensive and unprecedented effort to overturn the results of the presidential election.

As alleged in the Article of Impeachment and described in this report, President Trump has acted in a manner grossly incompatible with self-governance and the rule of law. His continued hold on the Office of the Presidency, even for only a few more days, represents a clear and present danger to the United States.

President Trump has engaged in a prolonged effort to overturn the results of the 2020 presidential election and maintain his grip on power. He has spent months spreading disinformation about the results—falsely claiming that he "won by a landslide," that the election was being "stolen," and that the reported results are somehow fraudulent. He has stated that it would be illegitimate to accept the results of the election as certified by state officials and upheld by state and federal courts, and he has implied that accepting those results would pose an existential threat to the country, its democracy, and the freedoms of his political supporters. He has directly threatened government officials to "find" lost votes or face criminal penalties, encouraged his own Vice President to unlawfully overturn the election results and, ultimately, incited his supporters to take violent action and prevent the counting of the election results.

President Trump invited his political supporters to Washington, D.C. on January 6, 2021, the day fixed by law for the counting of electoral votes. The crowd that gathered in the Ellipse that morning was large, angry, and widely reported to be preparing for violent action. At that rally, the President delivered an incendiary speech to his supporters. Among other statements, President Trump reiterated false claims that "we won this election, and we won it by a landslide." He stated that "if you don't fight like hell, you're not going to have a country anymore." And then he exhorted his supporters to "walk down Pennsylvania Avenue" to prevent the Congress from confirming the election of "an illegitimate President."

These comments directly incited a violent attack on the Capitol that threatened the safety and lives of the Vice President, the Speaker of the House, and the President pro tempore of the Senate, the first three individuals in the line of succession to the presidency. The rioters attacked law enforcement officers, unleashed chaos and terror among Members and staffers and their families, occupied the Senate Chamber and Speaker Nancy Pelosi's office, ransacked other offices, vandalized government property, and succeeded in interfering with Congress's performance of its constitutional duty to count the electoral votes. Five people were killed, including a U.S. Capitol police officer, and more than fifty police officers were seriously injured.

It is indisputable that the President encouraged—and that his actions foreseeably resulted in—the terrorist attack that occurred. This alone would constitute grounds for impeachment. There is no place in our government for any officer, much less a President, who incites armed insurrection to overturn the results of our democratic elections.

Even after it became clear that a mob of his supporters had breached the Capitol perimeter and was violently attacking those inside, President Trump failed to take steps to stop the insurrection. While violent insurrectionists occupied parts of the Capitol, President Trump ignored or rejected repeated real-time entreaties from Speaker Nancy Pelosi and Senate Minority Leader Chuck Schumer to appeal to his followers to exit the Capitol. Instead, he continued to encourage his supporters and excoriated the Vice President for not "hav[ing] the courage to do what should have been done." He called at least one Republican Senator, not to check on his safety, but to ask for additional delay to the certification of the election when the Congress reconvened. When he finally issued a public statement addressing the violence hours after it began, President Trump persisted in falsely asserting that "we had an election that was stolen from us," and he told the rioters, "[w]e love you, you're very special." And at the end of the day—when the extent of the insurrection and the damage to our nation was clear—he declared that "[t]hese are the things and events that happen when a sacred landslide election victory is so unceremoniously & viciously stripped away." President Trump concluded: "Remember this day forever!" Most recently, the President publicly denied responsibility for the attack, claiming his words were "totally appropriate."

The threat that manifested in the Capitol on January 6, 2021 is ongoing. The emergency is still with us. Reports suggest that the President's supporters are threatening additional violence in Washington, D.C. and in state capitals across the nation. The Fourteenth Amendment prohibits an officer of the United States who has "engaged in insurrection or rebellion" from "hold[ing] any office . . . under the United States." Yet, despite widespread and bipartisan calls for his immediate resignation, the President has refused to leave office. The Vice President has thus far failed to invoke the Twenty-fifth Amendment to remove the President from office. The House has taken every step short of impeachment to contain the danger. Now it is time to consider this last, grave, necessary step.

Impeachment is not a punishment of prior wrongs, but a protection against future evils. It is true that the President's remaining term is limited—but a President capable of fomenting a violent insurrection in the Capitol is capable of greater dangers still. He must be removed from office as swiftly as the Constitution allows. He must also be disqualified to prevent the recurrence of the extraordinary threat he presents. For these reasons, the House must impeach President Donald J. Trump.

I. Factual Background

The events surrounding the impeachable conduct occurred in plain sight, unfolded in real time, and demonstrate unequivocally that President Trump incited an insurrection that did harm to our national interest. President's Trump conduct on January 6, 2021 was not an isolated event. It spanned months, escalating after it became clear that he lost his bid for re-election, and culminating in the final rallying cry immediately preceding the insurrection that occurred. President Trump continued this course of conduct while the violence was ongoing and has, since that time, shown no remorse.

On the basis of these facts, it is indisputable that President Trump committed "high Crimes and Misdemeanors." The evidentiary record available to date bearing on this conduct is set forth in the Appendix.

A. Conduct Leading Up to January 6, 2021

In the months leading up to January 6, 2021 President Trump engaged in a course of conduct designed to encourage and provoke his supporters to gather in Washington, D.C. and obstruct the process of the electoral votes that would confirm his defeat. That conduct spanned months and included frivolous and harassing lawsuits, direct threats to state and local officials, and false public statements to his supporters, all in an effort to incite his supporters into believing it was their patriotic duty to attack Congress and prevent the peaceful transition of power.

In the aftermath of the 2020 election, President Trump took aggressive steps to overturn its outcome and undermine public confidence in the results. The President and his allies filed sixty-two separate lawsuits across federal and state courts contesting every aspect of the election.[1] Every single lawsuit was dismissed, with the exception of one in Pennsylvania regarding ballot curing, and, even there, the court ruling did not in any way change the outcome of the election results in that state.[2] The President and those associated with him continue to press their increasingly baseless claims long after their factual and legal contentions had been repeatedly dismissed. These frivolous lawsuits were used by President Trump and his allies, not to identify legitimate concerns, but to undermine confidence in the results of the election, spread dangerous disinformation, and stoke false and wild conspiracy theories.

President Trump also asked his own Justice Department and the Federal Bureau of Investigation to investigate allegations of election fraud in an effort to change the outcome. At his direction, Attorney General William P. Barr authorized prosecutors "'to pursue substantial allegations of voting and vote tabulation irregularities prior to the certification of elections in your jurisdictions in certain cases,' particularly where the outcome of an election could be affected."[3]

---

[1] William Cummings, et al., *By the numbers: President Donald Trump's failed efforts to overturn the election*, USA Today (Jan. 6, 2021).

[2] *Id.*

[3] Matt Zapotosky & Tom Hamburger, *Federal prosecutors assigned to monitor election malfeasance tell Barr they see no evidence of substantial irregularities*, Wash. Post (Nov. 13, 2020).

That effort, too, failed. On November 13th, 2020, Assistant U.S. Attorneys in fifteen different federal court districts urged the Attorney General to cease investigations into "vote tabulation irregularities," based on a lack of evidence of "any substantial anomalies."[4] These officials further explained that, in the places where they served as district election officers, there was no evidence of the kind of fraud that Attorney General Barr's memo had highlighted and the "policy change was not based in fact."[5] In other words, there was no basis to investigate fraud in the election. Although the Attorney General pursued other investigations into the election results at the President's direction for some time, he ultimately confirmed on December 1, 2020 that "the U.S. Justice Department had uncovered no evidence of widespread voter fraud that could change the outcome of the 2020 election."[6]

Despite the across-the-board failure of the President's attempted lawsuits, and the lack of any meaningful evidence of fraud uncovered after multiple investigations by both DOJ and the FBI, President Trump still continued—without any evidentiary basis—to spread disinformation that he had won the election. This was part of his ongoing attempt to subvert its results, even urging public officials to "find the fraud" and threatening them if they failed to do so.

President Trump was especially fixated on Georgia. After Election Day, the state of Georgia's county canvass results showed that President Trump lost the election in Georgia by approximately 14,000 votes.[7] After an audit, the tally showed that President Trump had lost Georgia by more than 12,000 votes. As permitted by Georgia law, the Trump campaign requested a recount.[8]

Under Georgia law, the Secretary of State was required to certify the results of the election on November 20, 2020, and the governor was then required to promptly certify the appointment of a slate of presidential electors in accordance with the election results. President Trump publicly exhorted both men not to do so. Secretary of State Brad Raffensperger nevertheless proceeded to certify the results on November 20, 2020, and Georgia Governor Brian Kemp duly certified the appointment of a slate of electors that same day.[9] The recount requested by the Trump campaign, which proceeded in parallel, was performed electronically pursuant to state law.[10] After the

---

[4] *Id.*

[5] *Id.*

[6] Michael Balsamo, *Disputing Trump, Barr says no widespread election fraud*, AP (Dec. 1, 2020). (Notably, On December 14, moments after counting in the Electoral College confirmed that President-elect Joe Biden had received over the 270 votes needed to secure his presidency, President Trump announced on Twitter that Mr. Barr would be leaving the administration).

[7] Christina A. Cassidy, *EXPLAINER: Is Georgia's upcoming ballot 'audit' a recount?*, AP (Nov. 12, 2020).

[8] *Risk-Limiting Audit Report, Georgia Presidential Contest, November 2020*, Georgia Sec. of State (Nov. 19, 2020) (Available at https://sos.ga.gov/admin/uploads/11.19_.20_Risk_Limiting_Audit_Report_Memo_1.pdf).

[9] Marshall Cohen et al, *Georgia's GOP governor and secretary of state certify Biden win, quashing Trump's longshot attempt to overturn results*, CNN (Nov. 20, 2020).

[10] David Morgan, *Georgia sets timeline for Trump-requested vote recount*, Reuters (Nov. 23, 2020).

recount, the vote count remained materially unchanged; Georgia recertified the election result on December 7, 2020.[11]

The final tally showed that President Trump lost the State of Georgia by 11,779 votes.[12] Georgia's slate of presidential electors then duly cast their votes on December 14, 2020, in accordance with the Electoral Count Act of 1887. During the post-election period, the Trump campaign and supporters of President Trump filed at least seven lawsuits in Georgia courts seeking to overturn the result in Georgia or otherwise challenge the conduct of the election, all of which were dismissed either by the court or voluntarily by the plaintiff.[13]

Throughout this process, President Trump publicly and privately attempted to impede Georgia officials. He disparaged Governor Kemp and Secretary of State Raffensperger for months, at one point calling the latter an "enemy of the people" for refusing to overturn the election.[14] Among other attempts, as reported on December 23, 2020, President Trump called one of Georgia's lead investigators, urging him to "find the fraud" and claiming that the official would be a "national hero" if he did so.[15] In addition, President Trump placed inappropriate pressure on the Office of the U.S. Attorney for the Northern District of Georgia.[16] U.S. Attorney Byung J. Pak abruptly resigned on January 5, 2020. It has since been reported that Mr. Pak was told by White House officials he needed to resign because the President was "furious" that Mr. Pak was not pursuing the President's groundless claims of widespread voter fraud in Georgia.[17]

On January 2, 2021, President Trump called Georgia state officials, including Secretary Raffensperger, in yet another attempt to reverse the outcome in that state. During the call, which was recorded by Mr. Raffensperger's office, President Trump directly urged Mr. Raffensperger to "find" enough votes to overturn the state's results and threatened him with criminal penalties if he failed to do so. Specifically, President Trump stated:

> [The Georgia ballots are totally] illegal — it is more illegal for you than it is for them because, you know, what they did and you're not reporting it. *That's a criminal, that's a criminal offense. And you can't let that happen. That's a big risk to you and to Ryan, your lawyer.* And that's a big risk. But they are shredding ballots, in my opinion, based on what I've heard. And they are removing machinery, and they're moving it as fast as they

[11] Richard Fausset & Nick Corasaniti, Georgia Recertifies Election Results, Affirming Biden's Victory, N. Y. Times (Dec. 7, 2020).

[12] Christina A. Cassidy, *EXPLAINER: Is Georgia's upcoming ballot 'audit' a recount?*, AP (Nov. 12, 2020).

[13] Pete Williams & Nicole Via y Rada, *Trump's election fight includes over 50 lawsuits. It's not going well.*, NBC (Nov. 23, 2020).

[14] Richard Fausset, *Georgia Republicans Contort Themselves to Avoid Trump's Fury*, N. Y. Times (Dec. 2, 2020).

[15] Amy Gardner, *'Find the fraud': Trump pressured a Georgia elections investigator in a separate call legal experts say could amount to obstruction*, Wash. Post (Jan. 9, 2021).

[16] Kelly Mena, *Wall Street Journal: White House pressured Georgia federal prosecutor to resign*, CNN (Jan. 9, 2021).

[17] Aruna Viswanatha et al., *White House Forced Georgia U.S. Attorney to Resign*, Wall Street Journal (Jan. 9, 2021).

can, both of which are criminal finds. And you can't let it happen, and you are letting it happen. You know, I mean, I'm notifying you that you're letting it happen. So look. *All I want to do is this. I just want to find 11,780 votes,* which is one more than we have because we won the state.[18]

While waging this pressure campaign against public officials, President Trump also spread inflammatory and inaccurate claims that he won the election on his social media and in his public appearances, all as part of his effort to subvert and obstruct the election outcome. For example, on December 13th, President Trump tweeted false claims that he had won the election "overwhelmingly" and that Democrats had committed "massive" fraud, stating in full:

> The RINOS that run the state voting apparatus have caused us this problem of allowing the Democrats to so blatantly cheat in their attempt to steal the election, *which we won overwhelmingly.* How dare they allow this massive and ridiculous Mail-In Voting to occur... […] ...Tens of millions of haphazardly ballots sent, with some people getting two, three, or four ballots. *We will never give up!*[19]

These public statements—espousing false theories of election fraud that had already been rejected by his own Justice Department—continued to escalate over the coming weeks. On December 18th, for example, President Trump urged his supporters and Republican Senators to "get tougher," tweeting "[w]e won the Presidential Election, by a lot. FIGHT FOR IT! Don't let them take it away," and adding on December 22nd "[t]he truth is we won the election by a landslide. We won it big."[20] The next week, President Trump falsely tweeted that the "United States had more votes than it had people voting, by a lot. This travesty cannot be allowed to stand. It was a Rigged Election, one not even fit for third world countries!"[21]

President Trump focused specifically on January 6, 2021. His messaging included a specific call to action: "Come to D.C. January 6th to 'StopTheSteal.'" On December 19th, for example, he tweeted: "Statistically impossible to have lost the 2020 Election. Big protest in D.C. on January 6th. … *Be there, will be wild!*"[22] He maintained this focus in the following weeks, including tweeting on January 1st "The BIG Protest Rally in Washington, D.C. will take place at

---

[18] Amy Gardner & Paulina Firozi, *Here's the full transcript and audio of the call between Trump and Raffensperger,* Wash. Post (Jan. 5, 2021) (emphasis added).

[19] Donald J. Trump (@realDonaldTrump), Twitter (Dec. 13, 2020, 5:15 PM) (online and searchable at http://www.trumptwitterarchive.com/archive) (emphasis added).

[20] *Id.* at (Dec. 18, 2020, 9:14 AM) (online and searchable at http://www.trumptwitterarchive.com/archive).; Donald Trump Vlog: *Contesting Election Results - December 22, 2020* (Dec. 22, 2020), Factbase Videos, available at https://www.youtube.com/watch?v=YJ8LfWC1Wks&feature=emb_logo.

[21] Donald J. Trump (@realDonaldTrump), Twitter (Dec. 30, 2020, 2:38 PM) (online and searchable at http://www.trumptwitterarchive.com/archive).

[22] *Id.* at (Dec. 19, 2020, 1:42 AM) (online and searchable at http://www.trumptwitterarchive.com/archive).

11:00 A.M. on January 6th. Locational details to follow. StopTheSteal!"[23]; the President even confirmed his own presence on that date, stating "I will be there! Historic day."[24]

In the days leading up to January 6th, President Trump escalated further, encouraging his supporters not just to show up in D.C., but specifically to obstruct the electoral count and the peaceful transition of power. On January 4th, for example, President Trump told his supporters at a Georgia rally: "Democrats are trying to steal the White House … [y]ou can't let it happen. You can't let it happen," and that "[T]hey're not taking this White House. *We're going to fight like hell*, I'll tell you right now."[25] And the day prior, President Trump further provoked his supporters by tweeting, among other comments, "Washington is being inundated with people who don't want to see an election victory stolen by emboldened Radical Left Democrats. Our Country has had enough, they won't take it anymore!"[26]

President Trump also began to spread the false claim that Vice President Pence had the unilateral authority to reject the results of the Electoral College, claiming, "If Mike Pence does the right thing we win the election … we become president and you are the happiest people. … Mike Pence is going to have to come through for us and if he doesn't, it's a sad day for our country."[27] To enhance pressure on his Vice President, President Trump repeatedly attacked him publicly and privately as disloyal for failing to take unconstitutional measures to alter the election outcome.[28]

As President Trump ramped up his rhetoric and false claims, his supporters were led to believe that the democratic process posed a threat to the country and required intervention.

B. The January 6, 2021 "Save America Rally"

By January 6th, President Trump had succeeded in creating a tinder box of thousands of supporters, riled up and ready to obstruct the electoral count if Vice President Pence refused to undertake unconstitutional action in his role as Presiding Officer at the Joint Session. In fact, the President tweeted twelve times on the morning of January 6th, continuing to spread false claims

---

[23] *Id.* at (Jan. 1, 2021, 2:23 PM) (online and searchable at http://www.trumptwitterarchive.com/archive).

[24] *Id.* at (Jan. 3, 2021, 10:27 AM) (online and searchable at http://www.trumptwitterarchive.com/archive).

[25] *Speech: Donald Trump Holds a Political Rally in Dalton, Georgia - January 4, 2021* (Jan. 4, 2021), Factbase Videos, available at https://www.youtube.com/watch?v=kL_IpqRf8RM;. *see also Speech: Donald Trump Holds a Political Rally in Valdosta, Georgia - December 5, 2020* (Dec. 5, 2020), Factbase Videos, available at https://www.youtube.com/watch?v=hKBZemnS1j4&feature=emb_logo.

[26] Donald J. Trump (@realDonaldTrump), Twitter (Jan. 5, 2021, 5:05 PM) (online and searchable at http://www.trumptwitterarchive.com/archive).

[27] Aaron Glantz, *Read Pence's full letter saying he can't claim 'unilateral authority' to reject electoral votes*, PBS (Jan. 6, 2021).

[28] Donald J. Trump (@realDonaldTrump), Twitter (Jan. 6, 2021, 1:00 AM) (online and searchable at http://www.trumptwitterarchive.com/archive).; *See also Id.* at (Jan. 6, 2021, 8:17 AM).

that the election was "rigged," and encouraging his supporters to "fight" and "be strong."[29] President Trump also urged Vice President Pence to act illegally before the electoral count began, tweeting at 8:17 AM on the morning of January 6, 2021, "States want to correct their votes, which they now know were based on irregularities and fraud, plus corrupt process never received legislative approval. All Mike Pence has to do is send them back to the States, AND WE WIN. Do it Mike, this is a time for extreme courage!"[30]

President Trump had also already scheduled a rally for the day that Congress was assembled to finalize the election results, set up within walking distance of the Capitol, dubbed the "Save America Rally." The title and location of the rally further underscored the President's messaging to his supporters that it was their patriotic duty to stop the electoral count.

The Save America Rally commenced at approximately 9:00 AM.[31] Shortly before the President spoke, his attorney Rudy Giuliani reiterated the President's false claims that the 2020 presidential election was not a "clean election," and ended by urging the crowd to "have trial by combat."[32] The President's son, Donald Trump Jr., also spoke, warning Republican congressmembers who did not support his father that *we're coming for you.*"[33]

At approximately 11:57 AM, the President addressed the crowd for over an hour, concluding at roughly 1:11 PM.[34] The President falsely insisted yet again that Democrats had "stolen" the election, and that his supporters instead should "fight much harder" to "stop the steal" and "take back our country" at the Capitol.[35] Although at one point he suggested that those marching to the Capitol should do so "peacefully," the overall tenor of his speech was menacing— and, as subsequent events showed, was understood by his supporters as such.

---

[29] *See, e.g.*, Donald J. Trump (@realDonaldTrump), Twitter (Jan. 6, 2021, 12:08 AM); *Id.* at (Jan. 6, 2021, 12:16:00 AM); *Id.* at (Jan. 6, 2021, 12:16:10 AM); *Id.* at (Jan. 6, 2021, 12:17:43 AM); *Id.* at (Jan. 6, 2021, 12:17:52 AM); *Id.* at (Jan. 6, 2021, 12:43 AM); *Id.* at (Jan. 6, 2021, 12:46 AM); *Id.* at (Jan. 6, 2021, 12:47 AM); *Id.* at (Jan. 6, 2021, 1:00 AM); *Id.* at (Jan. 6, 2021, 8:06 AM); *Id.* at (Jan. 6, 2021, 8:17 AM); *Id.* at (Jan. 6, 2021, 8:22 AM) (online and searchable at http://www.trumptwitterarchive.com/archive).

[30] *Id.* at (Jan. 6, 2021, 8:17 AM) (online and searchable at http://www.trumptwitterarchive.com/archive).

[31] Watch LIVE: Save America March at The Ellipse featuring President @realDonaldTrump, RSBN TV (Jan. 6, 2020) available at https://www.pscp.tv/w/1eaJbnwgERXJX?t=3h32m2s (hereinafter: "Save America March at the Ellipse Live Stream").

[32] Save America March at the Ellipse Live Stream; *see also* Rudy Giuliani Speech Transcript at Trump's Washington, D.C. Rally: Wants 'Trial by Combat, Rev (Jan. 6, 2021) ("If they ran such a clean election, they'd have you come in and look at the paper ballots. Who hides evidence? Criminals hide evidence. Not honest people. Over the next 10 days, we get to see the machines that are crooked, the ballots that are fraudulent, and if we're wrong, we will be made fools of. But if we're right, a lot of them will go to jail. Let's have trial by combat.").

[33] Maggie Haberman, *Trump Told Crowd, "You Will Never Take Back Our Country with Weakness,"* N. Y. Times (Jan. 6, 2021).

[34] Domenico Montanaro, *Timeline: How One Of The Darkest Days In American History Unfolded*, NPR (Jan..7, 2021); *see also* Save America March at the Ellipse Live Stream

[35] Maggie Haberman, *Trump Told Crowd, "You Will Never Take Back Our Country with Weakness.* N. Y. Times (Jan. 6, 2021).

The President also continued to insist that Vice President Pence act to overturn the election on his behalf: "All Vice-President Pence has to do is send it back to the States to recertify, and we become president, and you are the happiest people. . . . Mike Pence, I hope you're going to stand up for the good of our Constitution and for the good of our country. And if you're not, I'm going to be very disappointed in you. I will tell you right now. I'm not hearing good stories."[36]

The President even called out specific legislators, warning these elected officials to help in his efforts to overturn the election results or face consequences. Among other comments, he stated: "And we've got to get rid of the weak congresspeople, the ones that aren't any good, the Liz Cheney's of the world, we got to get rid of them."[37] His speech, in full, added additional such warnings, false claims, and encouragement to his supporters to take action, including the following:

> All of us here today do not want to see our election victory *stolen by [sic] bold and radical left Democrats* which is what they are doing and stolen by the fake news media. That is what they have done and what they are doing. We will never give up. *We will never concede*. It doesn't happen. You don't concede when there's theft involved.... Our country has had enough. *We will not take it anymore, and that is what this is all about. ... And to use a favorite term that all of you people really came up with, we will stop the steal*. ... We will not let them silence your voices. We're not going to let it happen.

> But just remember this, you're stronger, you're smarter. You've got more going than anybody and they try and demean everybody having to do with us and you're the real people. You're the people that built this nation. You're not the people that tore down our nation. ... Republicans are constantly fighting like a boxer with his hands tied behind his back. It's like a boxer. And we want to be so nice. We want to be so respectful of everybody, including bad people. We're going to have to fight much harder and Mike Pence is going to have to come through for us. If he doesn't, that will be a sad day for our country because you're sworn to uphold our constitution. Now it is up to Congress to confront this egregious assault on our democracy.

> After this, we're going to walk down and I'll be there with you. We're going to walk down. Anyone you want, but I think right here, *we're going to walk down to the Capitol*--And we're going to cheer on our brave senators and congressmen and women and *we're probably not going to be cheering so much for some of them. Because you'll never take back our country with weakness. You have to show strength and you have to be strong*.

> . . . I said something is wrong here, something is really wrong, can't have happened and we fight, *we fight like hell, and if you don't fight like hell you're not going to have a country anymore*. ... [W]e are going to try--give our Republicans, the weak ones because the strong ones don't need any of our help, *we're try--going to try and give them the kind*

[36] Julia Jacobo, *This is what Trump told supporters before many stormed Capitol Hill*, ABC News (Jan. 7, 2021).
[37] *Id.*

of pride and boldness that they need to take back our country. So let's walk down Pennsylvania Avenue.[38]

While President Trump was speaking, Vice President Pence issued a public letter in which he made clear that he would follow the Constitution and the law despite President Trump's urgings to the contrary. "I do not believe," he wrote, "that the Founders of our country intended to invest the vice president with unilateral authority to decide which electoral votes should be counted during the Joint Session of Congress, and no vice president in American history has ever asserted such authority. . . . It is my considered judgment that my oath to support and defend the Constitution constrains me from claiming unilateral authority to determine which electoral votes should be counted and which should not."[39]

As soon as President Trump concluded his speech, thousands of attendees marched down Pennsylvania Avenue toward Capitol Hill—just as President Trump had instructed them.

C. The Attack on the Capitol

On January 6, at 1:00 PM, as the President's rally was drawing to a close, the House and the Senate met in a Joint Session of Congress, with the Vice President presiding, to count the Electoral College's votes for who "shall be the President. " as required by the Twelfth Amendment and the Electoral Count Act.[40] By around 2:00 PM, the supporters attending the rally had surged toward the Capitol and were attempting to breach its security barriers, requiring the Capitol Police to issue a number of security orders including one at 2:03 PM ordering an internal relocation of those in the Cannon House Office Building.[41]

At 2:02 PM, less than an hour after the President concluded his speech, reports confirmed that his supporters were attempting to breach the Capitol itself.[42] Within minutes, Members of the House and Senate were told that the Capitol was in lockdown and were alerted to stay away from doors and windows.[43] By 2:07 PM, the mob had breached the steps on the east side of the Capitol

---

[38] Julia Jacobo, *This is what Trump told supporters before many stormed Capitol Hill*, ABC News (Jan. 7, 2021) (emphasis added).

[39] Mike Pence (@Mike_Pence), Twitter (Jan. 6, 2021, 1:02 PM).

[40] Domenico Montanaro, *Timeline: How One Of The Darkest Days In American History Unfolded*, NPR (Jan. 7, 2021).

[41] Chris Marquette et al., *Pro-Trump protesters storm Capitol during Electoral College certification, causing lockdown*, Roll Call (Jan. 6, 2021) (At 1:22 PM Capitol Police ordered the evacuation of the Cannon House Office Building and at 1:47 PM the department announced the evacuation was all clear. However, by 2:03 PM Capitol Police issued its relocation order for Cannon House Office Building and by 2:18 PM Capitol Police had issued its lockdown of the Capitol complex); *See also* Zolan Kanno-Youngs et al., *As House Was Breached, a Fear 'We'd Have to Fight' to Get Out*, N. Y. Times (Jan. 6, 2021).

[42] Igor Bobic (@igorbobic), Twitter (Jan. 6, 2021, 2:02PM), https://twitter.com/igorbobic/status/1346895006263631872?s=20.

[43] *Id.* at (Jan. 6, 2021, 2:05 PM), https://twitter.com/igorbobic/status/1346895569277628417.

and, minutes later, were inside the Capitol itself.[44] From that time, the insurrectionists desecrated the Capitol including by, among other acts, ransacking and looting Member offices, stealing and destroying electronics, government property, and sensitive materials, and engaging in violence, which eventually resulted in at least five deaths. The following is a summary of these acts as recounted in criminal complaints, eyewitness experiences, and firsthand photographs and videos of the events.

To enter the Capitol, the insurrectionists overwhelmed Capitol Police, scaled walls, used makeshift ladders, shattered windows, and overran barricades.[45] Although Capitol Police locked the gallery and floor doors and Members and staff barricaded themselves in offices, the mob stormed Member offices, vandalizing and smashing property, overturning furniture, and, in some cases, stealing electronics.[46] The day after the attack, the Justice Department noted that the thefts "could have potential national security equities."[47] The full impact of hundreds of violent rioters with smartphones rampaging unsupervised in the Capitol, with direct access to electronics, computers, and networks, is not yet known.

Insurrectionists also severely damaged the building itself. They left bullet marks in the building walls, looted art, destroyed monuments, including a commemorative display honoring late congressman John Lewis, smeared their feces in several hallways, and fatally injured a Capitol Police officer.[48] Several brandished the Confederate battle flag and extremist paraphernalia.[49]

By approximately 2:45 PM, insurrectionists had breached the House and Senate floors and began posing for photographs, including on the dais where Vice President Mike Pence had been presiding just moments before.[50] Other images showed rioters smoking marijuana in Capitol rooms.[51] The insurrectionists had, among their gear and weaponry, bullet-proof vests, zip ties used for handcuffs, metal knuckles, sticks and poles, knives, and firearms; in total, at least six handguns

---

[44] Domenico Montanaro, *Timeline: How One Of The Darkest Days In American History Unfolded*, NPR (Jan. 7, 2021).

[45] Marc Fisher et al., *The four-hour insurrection*, Wash. Post (Jan. 7, 2021).

[46] Jack Brewster & Andrew Solender, *Clyburn's Ipad, Laptop From Pelosi's Office: Items Stolen, Destroyed In Capitol Attack*, Forbes (Jan. 7, 2021); Kel McClanahan, *The MAGA Insurrection in the Capitol Created a Huge New National-Security Threat*, Daily Beast (Jan. 8, 2021); Senator Jeff Merkley (@SenJeffMerkley), Twitter (Jan. 6, 2021 11:36 PM).

[47] Natasha Bertrand, *Justice Department warns of national security fallout from Capitol Hill insurrection*, POLITICO (Jan. 7, 2021).

[48] *See* Chris Sommerfeldt, *Pro-Trump rioters smeared poop in U.S. Capitol hallways during belligerent attack*, NY Daily News (Jan. 7, 2021); Sarah Bahr, *Curators Scour Capitol for Damage to the Building or Its Art*, N. Y. Times (Jan. 7, 2021); Zack Budryk, *Hoyer says rioters destroyed display commemorating John Lewis*, The Hill (Jan. 7, 2021); Chelsea Stahl, *Jan. 7 highlights and analysis of unrest in Washington, D.C.*, NBC (Jan. 8, 2021); Lauren Egan, *Capitol reels from damage and destruction left by violent rioters*, NBC (Jan. 7, 2021).

[49] Julia Jacobo, *A visual timeline on how the attack on Capitol Hill unfolded*, ABC News (Jan. 10, 2021).

[50] Igor Bobic (@igorbobic), Twitter (Jan. 6, 2021, 2:47 PM), https://twitter.com/igorbobic/status/1346906369232920576.

[51] Sarah Bahr, *Curators Scour Capitol for Damage to the Building or Its Art*, N. Y. Times (Jan. 7, 2021).

were recovered from subsequent arrests.[52] Videos confirmed that these insurrectionists were openly threatening specific Members of Congress. For example, some of the attackers said, "Tell Pelosi we're coming for that [expletive]."[53]

Members of this mob also made clear that they attacked the Capitol because they believed the President had directed them to. One, individual, Jacob Chansley, who wore a "bearskin headdress" and "carried a spear, approximately 6 feet in length,"[54] later told police that he came as part of a group effort at the request of the President.[55] Another, Derrick Evans, had posted on social media at 12:08 AM on January 6th that he was going to D.C. to "#StopTheSteal," in response to the President's tweet.[56] Similarly, a livestream video from inside the Capitol revealed an insurrectionist explaining, "[o]ur president wants us here. … *We wait and take orders from our president*."[57]

Outside, the mob erected a gallows, disabled police vehicles, and left threatening messages to Members.[58] Police discovered in a nearby pickup truck—which was later found to belong to one of the President's supporters traveling from Alabama[59]—eleven "mason jars containing an unknown liquid," "cloth rags," and "lighters," which appeared to be "consistent with components for an explosive or incendiary device known as a 'Molotov Cocktail.'"[60] The truck additionally contained a black handgun and an M4 carbine assault rifle with loaded ammunition magazines.[61] The Capitol Police Hazardous Materials Response Team also confirmed two devices that were

---

[52] Officer Dallan Haynes Statement of Facts (Jan. 7, 2021) at 2, available at https://www.justice.gov/opa/press-release/file/1351686/download; Officer Christopher Frank Affidavit (Jan. 6, 2021) at 1, available at https://beta.documentcloud.org/documents/20446048-sinclair_affidavit; Officer Alexandria Sims Affidavit (Jan. 7, 2021) at 1, available at https://assets.documentcloud.org/documents/20446053/blair_affidavit.pdf; Special Agent Lawrence Anyaso Affidavit (Jan. 7, 2021) at 1, available at https://www.justice.gov/opa/press-release/file/1351661/download; DC Police Department (@DCPoliceDept), Twitter (Jan. 7, 2021, 1:52 PM), https://twitter.com/DCPoliceDept/status/1347254914993549312.

[53] Matthew S. Schwartz, *As Inauguration Nears, Concern Of More Violence Grows*, NPR (Jan. 9, 2021).

[54] Special Agent James Soltes Affidavit (Jan. 8, 2021) at 1, available at https://www.justice.gov/usao-dc/press-release/file/1351941/download.

[55] *Id.* at 3.

[56] Special Agent David J. Dimarco Affidavit (Jan. 8, 2021) ¶ 13, available at https://www.justice.gov/usao-dc/press-release/file/1351946/download.

[57] Dan Barry et al., *'Our President Wants Us Here': The Mob That Stormed the Capitol*, N. Y. Times (Jan. 9, 2021) (emphasis added).

[58] Azi Paybarah and Brent Lewis, Stunning Images as a Mob Storms the U.S. Capitol, N. Y. Times (Jan. 6, 2021).

[59] Carol Robinson, *Lonnie Coffman, Alabama man arrested at DC riot, had homemade napalm in Mason jars, feds say*, AL (Jan. 8, 2021).

[60] Anyaso Aff. at 1-2.

[61] Anyaso Aff. at 1.

"hazardous and could cause great harm to public safety" near the Capitol, and further reports confirmed a "hooded figure with a pipe bomb."[62]

Over 50 police officers were injured while defending the Capitol. In one instance, President Trump's supporters grabbed a police officer by the helmet and dragged him down the stairs. Others "kicked and punched the officer, and one man even bashed the prone figure repeatedly with a pole flying an American flag."[63] One officer, Brian Sicknick, died the following day from injuries suffered during the attack.[64] As of January 10th, at least 90 had been arrested, with more arrests expected.[65]

In the midst of this violence, the Secret Service evacuated Vice President Pence from the Senate floor, and Capitol Police attempted to evacuate or safely secure Members of Congress and their staff. Members were instructed to remove their identification pins in order to avoid targeted attacks. Gas masks were dispersed, and Members were ordered to shelter in place, instructed to stay under their desks or lie face down on the floor for their protection, or escorted by armed Capitol Police out of the building.[66]

Members have spoken publicly about the harrowing experience.[67] Representative Jamie Raskin asked his chief of staff to "protect [two of his visiting family members] with her life," as she stood guard at the door clutching a fire iron.[68] Representative Jason Crow, said that he had not been in a similar situation since serving in Afghanistan and described the chaos on the House floor: "[T]he police weren't able to get us out so they actually closed and locked the doors and started to take furniture and barricade the doors and the windows with furniture as the mob tried to ram them down and was breaking through the windows."[69] Representative Susan Wild, described hearing gun shots at approximately 3:00 PM and then Capitol Police screaming "Get down! Get down!", as she crawled on her hands and knees through the gallery, witnessing her colleagues making

---

[62] *Statement of Steven Sund, Chief of Police, Regarding the Events of January 6, 2021,* United States Capitol Police (Jan. 7, 2021), available at https://www.uscp.gov/media-center/press-releases/statement-steven-sund-chief-police; DC Police Department (@DCPoliceDept), Twitter (Jan. 8, 2021, 10:52 AM), https://twitter.com/DCPoliceDept/status/1347571797429018625.,].

[63] Katie Shepherd, *Video shows Capitol mob dragging police officer down stairs. One rioter beat the officer with a pole flying the U.S. flag,* Wash. Post (Jan. 11, 2021)

[64] *Loss of USCP Officer Brian D. Sicknick,* United States Capitol Police (Jan. 7, 2021). On January 10, the Capitol Police reported the death of a second officer who was present at the insurrection. Per reports, he died by suicide. *See* Allison Klein and Rebecca Tan, *Capitol Police officer who was on duty during the riot has died by suicide, his family says,* Wash. Post (Jan. 11, 2021).

[65] Michael Biesecker, *Records show fervent Trump fans fueled US Capitol takeover,* AP (Jan. 11, 2021).

[66] *See e.g.* Marc Fisher et al., *The four-hour insurrection,* Wash. Post (Jan. 7, 2021); Tasneem Nashrulla, Members Of Congress Described What It Was Like When A Pro-Trump Mob Stormed The Capitol, Buzzfeed (Jan. 6, 2021).

[67] Tasneem Nashrulla, Members Of Congress Described What It Was Like When A Pro-Trump Mob Stormed The Capitol, Buzzfeed (Jan. 6, 2021).

[68] John Hendrickson, *Jamie Raskin Lost His Son. Then He Fled a Mob.,* The Atlantic (Jan. 8, 2021).

[69] *Lawmaker describes moment captured in dramatic photo,* CNN (Jan. 6, 2021), available at https://www.youtube.com/watch?v=cufftGM8040.).

phone calls to loved ones.[70] Representative Dan Kildee described in real-time what was happening, "I am in the House Chambers. We have been instructed to lie down on the floor and put on our gas masks. Chamber security and Capitol Police have their guns drawn as protesters bang on the front door of the chamber."[71]

Other Members also described the confusion and chaos as the siege closed in on the House floor. Representative Pramila Jayapal recounted how "Capitol police with us seemed very confused about who had the key to the doors. They were closed, but we weren't sure if they were locked, and we were yelling, "Lock the doors! Lock the doors!"[72] We heard shots being fired, presumably into the chamber." She noted that took more than an hour and half for Members sitting in the gallery to evacuate: "Before we knew it, everyone on the floor below us had been removed, and … we were still there. And it didn't look like anyone was coming to get us."[73]

Many Members and staff were left traumatized by the experience. Representative Nancy Mace "felt unsafe returning to her hotel. What if rioters, who had just stormed and overtaken the Capitol building, were staying at her hotel? … She'd spent Wednesday huddled in someone's corner office, then stuck in a tunnel, then hunkered in her office with the lights off, her children texting her with worry."[74]

D. President Trump's Response to the Insurrection

Although the insurrection began immediately following the conclusion of his speech, President Trump did not swiftly denounce the violence, or order his supporters to lay down their arms. To the contrary, as he watched the violence unfold on television, President Trump was reportedly "borderline enthusiastic because it meant the certification was being derailed."[75] President Trump's reaction "genuinely freaked people out."[76] Senator Ben Sasse relayed a conversation with senior White House officials that President Trump was "walking around the

---

[70] Rose Minutaglio, *Rep. Susan Wild On The 'Sheer Panic' She Felt In That Viral Photo*, Elle (Jan. 7, 2021) ("I need to talk to my kids, I thought to myself, because I may never talk to them again. I FaceTimed my 27-year-old son, Clay, and my 24-year-old daughter, Adrienne, to let them know I was staying as safe as possible and that I would be okay. Clay said, 'We hear gunshots and breaking glass in the background. How can you say you're okay?' Something about that call prompted a panic inside me. My heart began to pound. I felt paralyzed. … The door was still barricaded and it sounded like bullets were ricocheting in the chamber. … Sheer panic.) (emphasis added).

[71] Rep. Dan Killdee (@RepDanKildee), Twitter (Jan. 6, 2021, 2:52 PM) https://twitter.com/RepDanKildee/status/1346907565482004495

[72] Rebecca Traister, 'It Was No Accident' Congresswoman Pramila Jayapal on surviving the siege, The Cut (Jan. 8, 2021).

[73] *Id.* 1

[74] Jennifer Berry & Thomas Novelly, Nancy Mace's first 100 hours in Congress: threats, violence and challenging Trump, The Post and Courier (Jan. 7, 2021).

[75] Kaitlan Collins (@kaitlancollins), Twitter (Jan. 6, 2021, 10:34 PM), https://twitter.com/kaitlancollins/status/1347023890959228933.

[76] *Id.*

White House confused about why other people on his team weren't as excited as he was as you had rioters pushing against Capitol Police trying to get into the building."[77] He was "delighted."[78]

And while the Senators were in lockdown, President Trump called Senator Mike Lee—apparently trying to reach Senator Tommy Tuberville instead. The President did so not to check the Senators' well-being or assess the security threats, but instead, like the mob itself, to disrupt the peaceful transition of power.[79] He encouraged Senator Tuberville to object and delay further the counting of electoral votes.[80]

The President's public statements were no better. Rather than defend the Capitol, comfort the American people, or urge his supporters to stand down, at the start of the siege, he retweeted at 1:49 PM a video of the rally, which included his previous statements that: "our country has had enough. We will not take it anymore and that's what this is all about. To use a favorite term that all of you came up with, we will stop the steal. . . You'll never take back our country with weakness. You have to show strength, and you have to be strong."[81]

By 2:20 PM, the nation saw on live television that the armed mob had overrun the Capitol, causing both the House and the Senate to recess prematurely[82] and flee their respective chambers in fear of their lives. Yet, even then, the President continued to affirm the insurrection's mission by attacking Vice President Pence for refusing to obstruct the process, tweeting at 2:24 PM:

> ***Mike Pence didn't have the courage to do what should have been done to protect our Country and our Constitution***, giving States a chance to certify a corrected set of facts, not the fraudulent or inaccurate ones which they were asked to previously certify. USA demands the truth![83]

Later video would emerge of insurrectionists inside the Capitol *chanting "Hang Mike Pence!"[84]*

---

[77] Andrew Prokop, *Republican senator: White House aides say Trump was "delighted" as Capitol was stormed*, Vox (Jan. 8, 2021).

[78] *Id.*

[79] Sunlen Serfaty et al., *As riot raged at Capitol, Trump tried to call senators to overturn election*, CNN (Jan. 8, 2021).

[80] *Id.* (Further, later that night, President Trump's lawyer Rudolph Giuliani tried to take advantage of the chaos by following up on President Trump's call. He left a message with Senator Tuberville to continue to object "so that we get ourselves into tomorrow.")

[81] Julia Jacobo, *This is what Trump told supporters before many stormed Capitol Hill*, ABC News (Jan. 7, 2021).

[82] Sonam Sheth, *House and Senate abruptly go into recess after Trump-supporting rioters storm the Capitol building*, Business Insider (Jan. 6, 2021).

[83] Donald J. Trump (@realDonaldTrump), Twitter (Jan. 6, 2021, 2:24 PM) (online and searchable at http://www.trumptwitterarchive.com/archive)

[84] Devlin Barrett et al., *FBI focuses on whether some Capitol rioters intended to harm lawmakers or take hostages*, Wash. Post (Jan.8, 2021).

The insurrectionists also made clear that they intended to harm House Speaker Nancy Pelosi. Some yelled, "Tell Pelosi we're coming for that [expletive]."[85] Others roamed the Capitol halls chanting menacingly, "Where's Nancy? Where's Nancy?"[86]

Around this time, Members of the House and Senate from both parties confirmed that they had privately asked—or were publicly urging—the President to mobilize the National Guard and order his supporters to cease the violence and leave the Capitol.[87] For example, House Minority Leader Kevin McCarthy confirmed that he had "already talked to the President" on the phone and said: "I think we need to make a statement. Make sure that we can calm individuals down."[88] Former New Jersey Governor Chris Christie elaborated, the "[P]resident caused this protest to occur. He's the only one that can make it stop. … [W]hat the president has said is not good enough. The President has to come out and tell his supporters to leave the capitol grounds."[89] Representative Mike Gallagher also tweeted during the Capitol occupation, "Mr. President. You have got to stop this. You are the only person who can call this off."[90] Similarly, Mick Mulvaney, the President's former Acting Chief of Staff, tweeted, "The President's tweet is not enough. He can stop this now and needs to do exactly that. Tell these folks to go home."[91] After reaching out to Ivanka Trump, Senator Graham said the President's aides "were all trying to get him to speak out, to tell everyone to leave."[92] Even the President's Chief of Staff Mark Meadows was prompted to speak to him after aides said, "They are going to kill people."[93]

Not until 4:17 PM—over two hours after the initial breach and well into the siege—did the President release a scripted, pre-recorded video, which included a call for "peace" and "law and order" and finally told his supporters "you have to go home now." That video, though, continued to reiterate his claims of election fraud, stating that the election was "stolen from us." Moreover, the President included a clear message of support and love for these insurrectionists, who were *still* wreaking destruction inside the Capitol building, saying, "we love you, you're very special." President Trump told the insurrectionists:

[85] Matthew S. Schwartz, *As Inauguration Nears, Concern Of More Violence Grows*, NPR (Jan. 9, 2021).

[86] Karoun Demirjian et al., *Inside the Capitol siege: How barricaded lawmakers and aides sounded urgent pleas for help as police lost control*, Wash. Post (Jan. 10, 2021).

[87] *See e.g.,* Ashley Parker et al., *Six hours of paralysis: Inside Trump's failure to act after a mob stormed the Capitol*, Wash. Post (Jan. 11, 2021).

[88] *Trump doesn't ask backers to disperse after storming Capitol*, PBS (Jan. 6, 2021).

[89] *Chris Christie says Trump should tell protesters to leave Capitol*, ABC NEWS (Jan. 6, 2021) available at https://abcnews.go.com/US/video/chris-christie-trump-protesters-leave-capitol-750938176, 2021.

[90] Editorial, *Mike Gallagher is right: 'Call it off, Mr. President'*, Wisconsin State Journal (Jan. 6, 2021).

[91] Mick Mulvaney (@MickMulvaney), Twitter (Jan. 6, 2021, 3:01 PM), https://twitter.com/MickMulvaney/status/1346909665423196162.

[92] Ashley Parker et al., *Six hours of paralysis: Inside Trump's failure to act after a mob stormed the Capitol*, Wash. Post (Jan. 11, 2021).

[93] *Id.*

I know your pain. I know you're hurt. We had an election that was stolen from us. It was a landslide election and everyone knows it, especially the other side. But you have to go home now. We have to have peace. We have to have law and order. ... So go home. *We love you, you're very special. ... I know how you feel.* But go home and go home in peace.[94]

Despite the President's belatedly released video, the insurrection continued. In fact, the Capitol building was not secured until 5:34 PM, and Congress did not continue counting electoral votes until 8:00 PM.[95]

By the time the Capitol was secured and counting resumed, four of the insurrectionists have died. One was shot by Capitol Police as she tried to climb through a window in order to gain access to the House chamber, and three succumbed to medical emergencies suffered during the attack.[96] In addition, it was widely reported that many Capitol Police Officers had been injured by insurrectionist attacks, one of whom would die the following day.[97] Yet, at 6:01 PM, in the aftermath of this devastation, President Trump's statement to the public was not a condemnation of the violence. Rather, it was a message that justified his supporters' actions and reiterated his lies about the election. He tweeted: "These are the things and events that happen when a sacred landslide election victory is so unceremoniously & viciously stripped away from great patriots who have been badly & unfairly treated for so long,"[98] ending with: "*Remember this day forever!*"[99]

E. The Events of January 6th Were a Result of and Incited by the President's Course of Conduct

The timeline of events demonstrates that President Trump encouraged and incited the violent and seditious acts that occurred. Moreover, the lawlessness that resulted from President Trump's conduct was entirely foreseeable by the President.

President Trump openly acknowledged, in advance of the insurrection, that his statements had incited huge crowds to descend on D.C. On the eve of the event, President Trump publicly tweeted:

Washington is being inundated with people who don't want to see an election victory stolen by emboldened Radical Left Democrats. Our Country has had enough, they won't

---

[94] Donald J. Trump (@realDonaldTrump), Twitter (Jan. 6, 2021, 4:17 PM), (online and searchable at http://www.trumptwitterarchive.com/archive; *See also* Tony Keith, *Twitter 'locks' President Trump for 12 hours Wednesday evening*, KKTV (Jan. 6, 2021) (emphasis added).

[95] Ted Barrett et al., *US Capitol secured, 4 dead after rioters stormed the halls of Congress to block Biden's win*, CNN (Jan. 7, 2021).

[96] *Id.*

[97] *Loss of USCP Officer Brian D. Sicknick*, United States Capitol Police (Jan. 7, 2021).

[98] Donald J. Trump (@realDonaldTrump), Twitter (Jan. 6, 2021, 6:01 PM), (online and searchable at http://www.trumptwitterarchive.com/archive)

[99] *Id.* (emphasis added).

take it anymore! We hear you (and love you) from the Oval Office. MAKE AMERICA GREAT AGAIN... I hope the Democrats, and even more importantly, the weak and ineffective RINO section of the Republican Party, *are looking at the thousands of people pouring into D.C. They won't stand for a landslide election victory to be stolen.* @senatemajldr @JohnCornyn @SenJohnThune.[100]

In the days prior to the event, President Trump had likewise acknowledged his awareness of the masses gathered as a result of his prior statements. For example, in response to the President's tweet encouraging his supporters to come to D.C. on January 6th, a supporter confirmed, "[t]he calvary [sic] is coming, Mr. President!", to which President Trump responded directly: "A great honor!"[101] And, in response to reports that crowds were "descending" upon D.C., the President wrote: "we hear you (and love you) from the Oval Office."[102]

Moreover, President Trump had every reason to know that, incited by his statements, the thousands of people pouring into D.C. would engage in *actual* violence. As early as December 1st, elected officials warned President Trump of the consequences of his rhetoric. For example, Gabriel Sterling, an elected official in Georgia, cautioned President Trump regarding his public statements spreading false claims about the election: "Mr. President . . . Stop inspiring people to commit potential acts of violence. Someone's going to get hurt, someone's going to get shot, someone's going to get killed."[103]

In the days leading up to the January 6th rally, it was widely reported that militia groups, the Proud Boys—a group the President told to "stand back and stand by" during a presidential debate—and others Trump supporters had posted pictures with weaponry that they planned to bring to the Rally and use to storm and occupy the Capitol.[104]

For example, a member of the Red-State Secession group on Facebook posted on January 5, 2021: "If you are not prepared to use force to defend civilization, then be prepared to accept

---

[100] Donald J. Trump (@realDonaldTrump), Twitter (Jan. 5, 2021, 5:05 PM); Id. at (Jan. 5, 2021, 5:12 PM) (online and searchable at http://www.trumptwitterarchive.com/archive) (emphasis added).

[101] Ed Pilkington, *Incitement: a timeline of Trump's inflammatory rhetoric before the Capitol riot*, The Guardian (Jan. 7, 2021).

[102] Donald J. Trump (@realDonaldTrump), Twitter (Jan. 5, 2021, 5:05 PM), (online and searchable at http://www.trumptwitterarchive.com/archive).

[103] *Gabriel Sterling of Sec of State's Office Blasts Those Threatening Election Workers*, GPB (Dec. 1, 2020), available at https://www.youtube.com/watch?v=jLi-Yo6lucQ.1, 2020); *See also* Amy Gardner and Keith Newell, *'Someone's going to get killed': GOP election official in Georgia blames President Trump for fostering violent threats*, Wash. Post (Dec. 1, 2020); Matthew Brown, *Trump campaign lawyer stirs outrage by saying ex-cyber chief should be 'taken out at dawn and shot'*, USA Today (Dec. 1, 2020).

[104] David Smith et al., *Donald Trump refuses to condemn white supremacists at presidential debate*, The Guardian (Sep. 29, 2020); Craig Timberg & Drew Harwell, *Pro-Trump forums erupt with violent threats ahead of Wednesday's rally against the 2020 election*, Wash. Post (Jan. 5, 2021).

barbarism," to which dozens of people posted comments, including pictures of weaponry that they planned to bring to the President's rally on January 6th.[105]

In another thread on thedonald.win, responding to the President's tweets, discussion included how to most effectively sneak guns into Washington, including one individual writing: "Yes, it's illegal, but *this is war* and we're clearly in a post-legal phase of our society."[106]

One supporter wrote out an exact blueprint for the events that unfolded: "But on Jan 6, remember. . .Capital Building/Halls of Congress is ground zero. Jump the lines. Cross the roadblocks. Push past the robo cops. Don't let them usher/kettle us to any other "symbolic" monument. IMPORTANT. They need to hear our roar inside the chambers before the [expletive] begins."[107] Another wrote: "The capitol is our goal. Everything else is a distraction. Every corrupt member of congress locked in one room and surrounded by real Americans is an opportunity that will never present itself again."[108] Supporters even predicted that the President would not deploy the National Guard, allowing them to ambush the Capitol Police: "[Trump] can order the NAT guard to stand down if needed. unfortunately he has no control over the Capitol Police... but there are only around 2k of them and a lot are useless fat asses or girls."[109]

Whether or not President Trump was aware of these specific posts, it was widely reported and understood within the federal government that the crowd planning to attending the Save America Rally included many individuals who were armed, dangerous, and prepared to carry out violence. Indeed, the day before the rally, several people were even arrested, including on weapons-related charges, for assaulting a police officer and simple assault.[110] One such arrest was the leader of the Proud Boys for destroying a church's "Black Lives Matter" banner at an earlier pro-Trump post-election rally.[111] These arrests and reports prompted D.C. Mayor Muriel Bowser to caution residents to avoid the rally, even mobilizing city police.[112]

---

[105] Dan Barry and Sheera Frenkel, *'Be There. Will Be Wild!': Trump All but Circled the Date*, Wash. Post (Jan. 6, 2021).

[106] Craig Timberg & Drew Harwell, *Pro-Trump forums erupt with violent threats ahead of Wednesday's rally against the 2020 election*, Wash. Post (Jan. 5, 2021); *see also* Andrew Beaujon, *MAGA Geniuses Plot Takeover of US Capitol*, Washingtonian (Jan. 5, 2021) ("TheDonald.win's posters have discussed ways they might "occupy" or "storm" the US Capitol to make citizens' arrests of lawmakers who hold old-fashioned views like honoring state-certified election results.").

[107] *Are we allowed access to Capitol Hill offices and chambers on Jan. 6?*, THE DONALD,. (last visited Jan. 10, 2021).

[108] *The capitol is our goal. Everything else is a distraction. Every corrupt member of congress locked in one room and surrounded by real Americans is an opportunity that will never present itself again*, THE DONALD, (last visited Jan. 10, 2021).

[109] *This many patriots would storm the capitol if President Trump orders it on January 6th.*, THE DONALD, (last visited Jan. 10, 2021)

[110] Allan Smith, *D.C. Police make several arrests ahead of major pro-Trump election protests*, NBC (Jan. 6, 2021).

[111]*Judge bans Proud Boys leader from Washington, D.C., after arrest*, NBC (Jan. 5, 2021).

[112] Brandy Zadronzyny & Ben Collins, *Violent threats ripple through far-right internet forums ahead of protest*, NBC (Jan. 5, 2020).

In short, this was no ordinary political event and everyone, including the President and his own administration officials, knew it. The insurrectionists responded directly to specific calls to action by the President, repeated and amplified over weeks and weeks. Indeed, the Associated Press reported that "many of the rioters had taken to social media after the November election to retweet and parrot false claims by Trump that the vote had been stolen in a vast international conspiracy. Several had openly threatened violence against Democrats and Republicans they considered insufficiently loyal to the president."[113]

As the President's former Chief of Staff John Kelly explained on January 7th, "You know, the president knows who he's talking to when he tweets or when he makes statements. He knows who he's talking to. He knows what he wants them to do. And the fact that he said the things, he has been saying the things he has been saying since the election, and encouraging people, no surprise, again, at what happened yesterday."[114] Kelly added that, were he a member of the Cabinet, he would invoke the 25th Amendment to make the Vice President Pence the acting president.[115]

II.   The Need for the House to Impeach President Trump

For the reasons stated herein, the President's conduct easily meets the standard for committing an impeachable offense. Further, his prior and ongoing conduct confirm his imminent threat to our security and democracy if he remains in or holds any future office and, therefore, the House must impeach President Trump.

A. Standards for Impeachment

President Trump's unprecedented actions in inciting an insurrectionist assault on the United States Capitol on January 6, 2021, necessitate that the House act swiftly to address this impeachable conduct.

His conduct demonstrates and cautions that, if left in office—or if allowed to hold office in the future—he will be a clear and present danger to the very foundation of our constitutional order and the safety and security of our nation. Under these unprecedented and extraordinary circumstances, the House neither needs nor can it afford to resort to a lengthy impeachment proceeding. To the contrary, it is entirely within the power of the House under the Constitution to act quickly.

On December 15, 2019, the Committee on the Judiciary of the House of Representatives issued a report entitled "Impeachment of Donald J. Trump President of the United States."[116] As

---

[113] Michael Biesecker, *Records show fervent Trump fans fueled US Capitol takeover*, AP (Jan. 11, 2021).

[114] *John Kelly says he would vote to invoke 25th Amendment*, CNN (Jan. 6, 2021), available at https://www.youtube.com/watch?v=8UzqChhaTP8.

[115] *Id.*

[116] *See* H. Rept. 116-346. at 28-75.

that report explains, the House's authority to structure an impeachment is rooted in two provisions of Article I of the Constitution. *First*, Article I vests the House with the "sole Power of Impeachment."[117] It imposes no other requirements as to how the House must carry out that responsibility. *Second*, Article I further states that the House is empowered to "determine the Rules of its Proceedings."[118] Taken together, these provisions give the House sole discretion to determine the manner in which it will investigate, deliberate, and vote upon grounds for impeachment.

House precedent confirms that the House may proceed directly to consideration of articles of impeachment on the House floor. As *Jefferson's Manual* notes, "[i]n the House various events have been credited with setting an impeachment in motion," including charges made on the floor, resolutions introduced by Members, or "facts developed and reported by an investigating committee of the House."[119] Indeed, any Member can call up a resolution containing articles of impeachment on the floor as a question of the privileges of the House. The House can dispose of the resolution in several ways including by voting on the resolution directly.

In the past, the House has conducted an inquiry to investigate allegations of impeachable misconduct against the President of the United States before voting directly on whether to adopt articles of impeachment. The unprecedented role President Trump played in inciting an insurrectionist assault on the United States Capitol on January 6, 2021, however, has created extraordinary circumstances that both demand the House act swiftly and obviate the need for the House to conduct a lengthy inquiry into his conduct. The urgency of the situation—as well as the fact that the President's actions occurred in public, and many Members directly witnessed and were victim to the consequences of those actions—obviates the need for additional inquiry.[120]

B. Application of Impeachment Standards to President Trump's Conduct

As the Article of Impeachment sets forth, President Trump's conduct easily satisfies the standards for a high Crime and Misdemeanor.

1. The Article of Impeachment Charges an Impeachable Offense

The Committee on the Judiciary's December 15, 2019 report is incorporated herein by reference[121]

As discussed in the Committee's prior report, under that standard, there can be no doubt that President Trump has committed "high Crimes and Misdemeanors." On January 6, 2021, he

---

[117] U.S. CONST. art I, § 2, cl. 5.

[118] U.S. CONST. art. I, § 5, cl. 2.

[119] *Constitution, Jefferson's Manual, Rules of the House of Representatives of the United States*, H. Doc. No. 115-177 § 603 (2019 ed.) (hereinafter "*Jefferson's Manual*").

[120] Committees of Congress are continuing to investigate misconduct relating to President Trump's earlier efforts to interfere with the 2016 election and to consider related legislative reforms.

[121] *See* H. Rept. 116-346; H. Doc. 116-95.

incited a mob to violently besiege the Capitol while the House, Senate, and Vice President met in Joint Session to count the electoral votes. The President's conduct undermined our national security, threatened the integrity of our democratic system, interfered with the peaceful transition of power, and imperiled a coequal branch of government. Further, President Trump's acts of incitement on January 6, 2021 followed his prior efforts to subvert and obstruct the certification of the election results. As noted, those efforts include, but are not limited to, a call in which he urged the Georgia's Secretary of State, to "find" enough votes to overturn the Georgia Presidential election results and threatened state officials if they failed to accede to his demands.

As constitutional commentators from across the ideological spectrum have recognized, this conduct is unquestionably impeachable.[122] A President who incites violence against the Congress and three of the highest-level federal officials—and does so while Congress counts the electoral votes in an election that he lost—imperils the constitutional system. This offense is precisely the sort of conduct warranting impeachment and removal from office.

To the Framers, that conclusion would be self-evident. Their worldview was shaped by a study of classical history, as well as a lived experience of resistance and revolution. From that background emerged an exquisite sensitivity to the paired dangers of the mob and the demagogue, which they associated with "the threat of civil disorder and the early assumption of power by a dictator."[123] Shay's Rebellion in 1786 gave that concern heightened salience at the Constitutional Convention, where the Framers—fearful of unruly mobs—sought to restrain excesses of popular passion.[124] James Madison, in particular, worked hard "to avoid the fate of those 'ancient and modern confederacies,' which he believed had succumbed to rule by demagogues and mobs."[125] Several of the *Federalist Papers* similarly warned against demagogues who would aggrandize themselves, and threaten the young Republic, by stirring popular fury and delusion.[126] The generation that came of age in the eighteenth century was familiar with leaders who incited angry mobs and threatened constitutional stability. They would have immediately recognized President

---

[122] *See e.g.* Frank O. Bowman, III, *The Constitutional Case for Impeaching Donald Trump (Again)*, Just Security (Jan. 9, 2021); Dorf on Law (@dorfonlaw), Twitter (Jan. 6, 2021, 3:10 PM); Norman Eisen, The riot happened because the Senate acquitted Trump, Wash Post (Jan. 8, 2021); Noah Feldman, *I Testified at Trump's Last Impeachment. Impeach Him Again*, Bloomberg (Jan. 7, 2021); David Landau and Rosalind Dixon, *The 25th Amendment Can Remove Trump, but We Shouldn't Stop There*, N. Y. Times (Jan. 7, 2021); *Stanford Law's Michael McConnell on the 25th Amendment and Trump*, Stanford Law School (Jan. 7, 2021); Michael Stokes Paulsen, *The Constitutional and Moral Imperative of Immediate Impeachment*, The Bulwark (Jan. 8, 2021); David Priess & Jack Goldsmith, Can Trump Be Stopped?, Lawfare (Jan. 7, 2021); John Podhoretz, *Donald Trump Should Be Impeached and Removed from Office Tomorrow*, Commentary Magazine (Jan. 6, 2021); Melissa De Witte and Sharon Driscoll, *Stanford Scholars React to Capitol Hill Takeover*, Stanford News (Jan. 6, 2021); Ilya Somin, *A Qualified Defense of Impeaching Trump Again*, Reason (Jan. 6, 2021); Cass Sunstein, *Does the 25th Amendment Apply to Trump? Quite Possibly*, Bloomberg (Jan. 7, 2021); Laurence H. Tribe & Joshua Matz, *Yes, Congress should impeach Trump before he leaves office*, The Washington Post (Jan. 8, 2021); Keith E. Whittington, The conservative case for impeaching Trump now, Wash. Post (Jan. 7, 2021); ACLU Again Calls for Impeachment of President Trump, ACLU Press Release (Jan. 10, 2021) (https://www.aclunc.org/news/aclu-again-calls-impeachment-president-trump).

[123] *See* Bernard Bailyn, *The Ideological Origins of the American Revolution* 282 (1967).

[124] *See* Jeffrey Rosen, *American is Living James Madison's Nightmare*, The Atlantic (October 2018).

[125] *Id.*

[126] Alexander Hamilton, *The Federalist Papers: No. 1.*

Trump's conduct on January 6, 2021. And they would not hesitate to declare that a President who incites a mob to charge, breach, and desecrate the Capitol had committed an impeachable offense.

That is particularly true when the President engaged in such conduct while Congress met to count. As the House Judiciary Committee explained in its previous impeachment report, the Framers viewed an attack on democracy—and the integrity of the Electoral College process, in particular—as presenting a paradigm case for impeachment:

> The Framers also anticipated impeachment if a President placed his own interest in retaining power above the national interest in free and fair elections. Several delegates were explicit on this point when the topic arose at the Constitutional Convention. By then, the Framers had created the Electoral College. They were "satisfied with it as a tool for picking presidents but feared that individual electors might be intimidated or corrupted." Impeachment was their answer. William Davie led off the discussion, warning that a President who abused his office might seek to escape accountability by interfering with elections, sparing "no efforts or means whatever to get himself re-elected." Rendering the President ''impeachable whilst in office'' was thus "an essential security for the good behaviour of the Executive." The Constitution thereby ensured that corrupt Presidents could not avoid justice by subverting elections and remaining in office.

> George Mason built on Davie's position, directing attention to the Electoral College: "One objection agst. Electors was the danger of their being corrupted by the Candidates; & this furnished a peculiar reason in favor of impeachments whilst in office. Shall the man who has practised corruption & by that means procured his appointment in the first instance, be suffered to escape punishment, by repeating his guilt?" Mason's concern was straightforward. He feared that Presidents would win election by improperly influencing members of the Electoral College (e.g., by offering them bribes). If evidence of such wrongdoing came to light, it would be unthinkable to leave the President in office—especially given that he might seek to avoid punishment by corrupting the next election. In that circumstance, Mason concluded, the President should face impeachment and removal under the Constitution. Notably, Mason was not alone in this view. Speaking just a short while later, Gouverneur Morris emphatically agreed that "*the Executive ought therefore to be impeachable for . . . Corrupting his electors*" …

> When the President concludes that elections threaten his continued grasp on power, and therefore seeks to corrupt or interfere with them, he denies the very premise of our constitutional system. The American people choose their leaders; a President who wields

> power to destroy opponents or manipulate elections is a President
> who rejects democracy itself.[127]

Given the Framers' paramount concern for the integrity of the democratic process, and their fear that a President might seek to corrupt the Electoral College, there can be no doubt that President Trump committed "high Crimes and Misdemeanors" in unleashing a violent mob on the Capitol while Congress met to count Electoral College votes. Indeed, this timing was no coincidence: President Trump's acts of incitement on January 6, 2021 were inextricably linked to a broader course of conduct aimed at delegitimizing the election results, obstructing and subverting the electoral process, and sowing discord and confusion in the Nation's democratic system.

Yet another aspect of President Trump's conduct confirms that it ranks as impeachable: the existential threat it posed to the separation of powers. The Framers knew that "[t]he accumulation of all powers, legislative, executive, and judiciary, in the same hands, . . . may justly be pronounced the very definition of tyranny."[128] To protect liberty, they wrote a Constitution that creates a system of checks and balances within the federal government. Some of those rules are expressly enumerated in our founding charter; others are implied from its structure or from traditions of inter-branch relations. As our history makes clear, a President may be subject to impeachment for conduct that usurps and destroys core constitutional prerogatives of Congress or the Judiciary.[129] From that premise, it is obvious that the President commits an impeachable offense if he engages in conduct, such as inciting a violent attack upon the Capitol, that places legislators in mortal peril and forces them to hurriedly evacuate the legislative chamber. The separation of powers cannot function if the President incites violence against the Congress—and if the Congress must proceed in fear of a President who has demonstrated his willingness to endanger its very security.

Of course, it was not only Congress whose security President Trump put at risk on January 6, 2021. His own Vice President was presiding over the Joint Session and was endangered. President Trump's acts of incitement also harmed the national security of the United States—both by virtue of the intelligence risks resulting from a physical intrusion of the Capitol and by virtue of the signal it sent to the Nation's adversaries, foreign and domestic. This, too, supports the conclusion that President Trump's misconduct rises to the level of an impeachable offense: "Impeachment for betrayal of the Nation's interest—and especially for betrayal of national security—was hardly exotic to the Framers."[130]

For all these reasons, the conduct charged in the Article of Impeachment constitutes a "high Crime and Misdemeanor" under the Constitution. "There comes a point at which a president can properly be impeached for his statements"[131]—and that point is indisputably reached when the President incites an assault on the legislature amid the constitutional process for the transfer of power. Both as an abusive exercise of presidential power, and as an instance of gross misconduct

---

[127] *See* H. Rept. 116-346 at 52-53.

[128] James Madison, *The Federalist Papers: No. 47.*

[129] *See* H. Rept. 116-346 at 45-46; 145-148.

[130] *Id.* at 49.

[131] Laurence H. Tribe & Joshua Matz, *To End A Presidency: The Power of Impeachment* 8565 (2018).

implicating our system of government committed while occupying the office of presidency, it falls within any reasoned interpretation of "high Crimes and Misdemeanors."

2. President Trump Committed the Charged Impeachable Offense

On January 6, 2021, President Trump committed the impeachable offense of incitement of insurrection by willfully making statements that, in context, encouraged and foreseeably resulted in lawless action at the Capitol. As explained above, he set the stage for the Capitol attack in the months leading up to January 6th, and on that date, he exhorted the mob into a frenzy, aimed it like a loaded gun down Pennsylvania Avenue, and pulled the trigger. His statements and actions surrounding this act of incitement confirm the conduct charged in the article of impeachment.

President Trump expressly and impliedly encouraged his supporters to besiege the Capitol and engage in violent, unlawful conduct. The mob did not come together—united in purpose, mission, and plan—by accident. It did not engage in violence, or breach the Capitol's defenses, without encouragement and provocation from President Trump. To the contrary, since Election Day, President Trump has done everything in his power, including taking steps beyond his lawful authority, to convince his supporters that they are victims of the greatest electoral fraud in history. He has blamed this "fraud" on state officials, state courts, federal courts, the media, Congress, and election administrators. He has convinced many of his supporters, falsely, that they actually voted him back into power and that their votes—indeed, their fundamental rights—have fallen victim to an array of nefarious forces working against them. To that end, he has repeatedly called on his supporters to "step up & FIGHT BACK" to resist "the steal."[132] He has personally threatened election officials, including Georgia Secretary of State Raffensperger, if they do not "find" votes or take steps needed to overturn the popular will.[133] Following his lead, President Trump's supporters have engaged in harassment and violent threats—including calls for a senior official who oversaw the United States election infrastructure to be "taken out at dawn and shot."[134] The president's rhetoric led Gabriel Sterling, an election official in Georgia, to issue a prophetic warning in the aftermath of the election: "Mr. President . . . Stop inspiring people to commit potential acts of violence. Someone's going to get hurt, someone's going to get shot, someone's going to get killed."[135]

Having promoted the false belief that his supporters are victims of a historic fraud—one that threatened not only America, but also their very safety and that of their families—President Trump called them to a "Save America Rally." He planned that rally on the very same day that his

---

[132]Borzou Daragahi (@borzoi), Twitter (Nov. 5, 2020, 10:14 AM), https://twitter.com/borzou/status/1324369493901123584?s=20.; *see also Speech: Donald Trump Holds a Political Rally in Dalton, Georgia - January 4, 2021* (Jan. 4, 2021), Factbase Videos, available at https://www.youtube.com/watch?v=kL_IpqRf8RM.

[133] Amy Gardner, *'I just want to find 11,780 votes': In extraordinary hour-long call, Trump pressures Georgia secretary of state to recalculate the vote in his favor*, Wash. Post (Jan. 3, 2021).

[134] Matthew Brown, *Trump campaign lawyer stirs outrage by saying ex-cyber chief should be 'taken out at dawn and shot'*, USA Today (Dec. 1, 2020).

[135] *Gabriel Sterling of Sec of State's Office Blasts Those Threatening Election Workers*, GPB (Dec. 1, 2020), available at https://www.youtube.com/watch?v=jLi-Yo6IucQ.

supporters had been led to believe the Congress was assembled with Vice President Pence to carry out the final and most irreversible step of the conspiracy against them. In advance of the Rally, he told his supporters to prepare for a "Historic" and "wild" day: "Statistically impossible to have lost the 2020 Election. Big protest in D.C. on January 6th. Be there, will be wild!"[136] In response to a supporter claiming that "[t]he calvary [sic] is coming, Mr. President!", President Trump responded, "A great honor!"[137] And he made the target of his ire well-known: the Capitol and the officials meeting therein—including the Vice President, who he criticized publicly and privately as disloyal for failing to take unconstitutional measures to alter the election outcome.[138]

At the January 6th rally, the President's private lawyer, Rudy Giuliani took the stage and called for "trial by combat."[139] The President's son, Donald Trump Jr., warned Republican congressmembers who did not support his father that "we're coming for you."[140] When President Trump took the stage, his own address was riddled with statements calculated to toss a match into the powder keg he had created. He enflamed the crowd by repeating his election grievances. He directed their ire towards Congress, including by calling out specific legislators: "And we got to get rid of the weak congresspeople, the ones that aren't any good, the Liz Cheneys of the world, we got to get rid of them." He told them to "fight like Hell and if you don't fight like Hell, you're not going to have a country anymore." And finally, after riling up the crowd and giving them their marching orders, he aimed them at the Capitol: "After this, we're going to walk down and I'll be there with you. We're going to walk down. We're going to walk down any one you want, but I think right here."[141]

As multiple lawmakers have observed, there can be no doubt that President Trump expressly and impliedly inflamed his supporters, pointed them straight at the Capitol, and encouraged them to take extraordinary, violent measures in response to a supposed evil conspiracy against them unfolding at the Capitol. As Senator Susan Collins explained: "The president does bear responsibility for working up the crowd and inciting this mob."[142] Similarly, Senator Sasse has observed: "I think it's obvious that the president's conduct wasn't merely reckless and destructive. It was a flagrant dereliction of his duty to uphold and defend the Constitution."[143] And

---

[136] Dan Barry & Sheera Frenkel, *'Be There. Will Be Wild!': Trump All but Circled the Date*, N. Y. Times (Jan. 6, 2021).

[137] Ed Pilkington, Incitement: a timeline of Trump's inflammatory rhetoric before the Capitol riot, The Guardian (Jan. 7, 2021).

[138] Donald J. Trump Tweet(@realDonaldTrump), Twitter (Jan. 6, 2021, 1/6 1:00AM:00 AM) (online and searchable at http://www.trumptwitterarchive.com/archive); *See also Id.* at (Jan. 6, 2021 8:17 AM.).

[139] Natalie Colarossi, *Bar Association Urged to Disqualify Giuliani Over 'Trial by Combat' Speech Before D.C. Riot*, Newsweek (Jan. 9, 2021).

[140] Maggie Haberman, Trump Told Crowd, *"You Will Never Take Back Our Country with Weakness,"* N. Y. Times (Jan. 6, 2021).

[141] *Speech: Donald Trump Holds a Political Rally on The Ellipse - January 6, 2021*, Factbase Videos (Jan. 6, 2021), available at https://www.youtube.com/watch?v=RTK1lm1jk60&feature=emb_logo.

[142] Steve Mistler, *Susan Collins: Trump 'Does Bear Responsibility' For Insurrection*, Maine Public (Jan. 6, 2021).

[143] Steve Inskeep, *Ben Sasse Rips Trump For Stoking Mob, Calls Josh Hawley's Objection 'Really Dumbass'*, NPR (Jan. 8, 2021).

the President's own former Attorney General echoed, "orchestrating a mob to pressure Congress is inexcusable."[144]

In the days leading up to the Save America Rally, President Trump touted the "thousands of people pouring into D.C." who "won't stand for a landslide election victory being stolen."[145] Supporters of President Trump met across Washington, D.C., joined by his close allies, including General Michael Flynn and Roger Stone, and speakers rallied the crowd with calls of "We're not backing down anymore" and "It is time for war."[146] It was entirely foreseeable in this circumstance that the mob—fired up, some armed and armored, some with public plans for doing so—would engage in violence at the Capitol as an imminent result of President Trump's encouragement and incitement at the rally.

It was also widely reported that militia groups and members had posted pictures with weaponry that they planned to bring to the rally, and had posted numerous times about how to storm and occupy the Capitol.[147] Several people had been arrested, including on weapons-related charges, for assaulting a police officer and simple assault.[148] The leader of the Proud Boys, a group the President previously told to "stand back and stand by"[149] on national television, was arrested for destruction of church property.[150] Recognizing the potential for violence, D.C. Mayor Muriel Bowser asked residents to stay away from the downtown area where the Rally would take place on Tuesday and Wednesday, and mobilized every city police officer.[151]

· These events also make clear that President Trump acted willfully. He actively encouraged the mob to besiege the Capitol in defense of his supposed electoral victory. In context, it was readily foreseeable that this would result in violence and lawless action. And it did, in fact, have that result. Given all that, there can be no serious doubt that President Trump intended these reasonably foreseeable results encouraged by his own conduct. He may not have anticipated every detail, but any reasonable person would understand that inflaming a mob containing armed, angry supporters, and then directing them towards the Capitol with the goal of "fighting like Hell" and thwarting a supposed massive electoral conspiracy would result in violence and destruction. Indeed, the contrary inference—that the President accidentally incited the mob to violence, and

---

[144] Orion Rummler, *Barr condemns Trump: "Orchestrating a mob to pressure Congress is inexcusable"*, Axios (Jan. 7, 2021).

[145] Donald J. Trump Tweet, (@realDonald Trump), Twitter (Jan. 5, 2021, 5:12 pm) (online and searchable at http://www.thetrumparchivetrumptwitterarchive.com/).

[146] Dan Barry et al., *'Our President Wants Us Here': The Mob That Stormed the Capitol*, N. Y. Times (Jan. 9, 2021).

[147] Craig Timberg & Drew Harwell, Pro-Trump forums erupt with violent threats ahead of Wednesday's rally against the 2020 election, Wash. Post (Jan. 5, 2021)

[148] Allan Smith, D.C. Police make several arrests ahead of major pro-Trump election protests, NBC (Jan. 6, 2021).

[149] *'Proud Boys, stand back and stand by': Trump doesn't condemn white supremacists at debate,* Wash. Post (Sep. 29, 2020).

[150] *Judge bans Proud Boys leader from Washington, D.C., after arrest, NBC (Jan. 5, 2021).*

[151] Brandy Zadronzyny & Ben Collins, *Violent threats ripple through far-right internet forums ahead of protest*, NBC (Jan. 5, 2021).

that he was accordingly shocked and dismayed by the mayhem it caused—is squarely inconsistent with the facts.

      That is evident, first and foremost, in how President Trump acted after the Capitol came under attack. While his supporters undertook a hostile occupation and ransacking of the Capitol—and after reports of gunshots and violence in the Capitol had become public on national television[152]—the President made no effort to quell the violence and destruction. Just minutes after the Sergeant at Arms announced that the Capitol had been reclaimed from the mob, and much of the destruction had occurred, he tweeted: "These are the things and events that happen when a sacred landslide election victory is so unceremoniously & viciously stripped away from great patriots who have been badly & unfairly treated for so long."[153] There was no denunciation of what had occurred, no urgent plea that his supporters lay down their arms, no national statement.[154] Instead, as Senator Sasse relayed from a conversation with senior White House officials, President Trump was "walking around the White House confused about why other people on his team weren't as excited as he was as you had rioters pushing against Capitol Police trying to get into the building."[155] He was "delighted."[156] And while the Senators were in lockdown, President Trump called one of them, not to check on his wellbeing or assess security risks, rather to encourage the Senator to object to the Electoral College vote.[157]

      The President's statements during the assault similarly confirm his intent. He tweeted multiple times, first to criticize the Vice President for not having "the courage to do what should have been done to protect our Country and our Constitution."[158] Next, still not calling for the mob to leave the Capitol, or for a massive deployment of force to retake the building, he issued two vague calls for his supporters to "stay peaceful" and "remain peaceful" despite overwhelming, public evidence that the mob was actively engaging in violence and destruction inside the Capitol.[159] And finally, well into the siege, he released a video in which he again reiterated his claims of election fraud and said that the election that was "stolen from us." While this video included a weak call for "peace" and "law and order," he also told his supporters—a band of whom

---

[152] CBS News (@CBSNews), Twitter (Jan. 6, 2021 3:56 PM), https://twitter.com/CBSNews/status/1346923577245896705; Rep. Elaine Luria (@RepElaineLuria), Twitter (Jan. 6, 2021, 1:46 PM), https://twitter.com/RepElaineLuria/status/1346890833266683904.

[153] *Twitter locks Trump's account after he encouraged his supporters to 'remember this day.'*, N. Y. Times (Jan. 8, 2021).

[154] Michael Levenson, *Today's Rampage at the Capitol, as It Happened*, N. Y. Times (Jan. 6, 2021).

[155] Andrew Prokop, Republican senator: White House aides say Trump was "delighted" as Capitol was stormed, Vox (Jan. 8, 2021).

[156] *Id.*

[157] Sunlen Serfaty et al., *As riot raged at Capitol, Trump tried to call senators to overturn election*, CNN (Jan. 8, 2021).

[158] Donald J. Trump (@realDonaldTrump), Twitter (Jan. 6, 2021, 2:24 PM) (online and searchable at http://www.trumptwitterarchive.com/archive).

[159] Donald J. Trump (@realDonaldTrump), Twitter (Jan. 6, 2021, 2:38 PM); *Id.* at (Jan. 6, 2021, 3:13 PM) (online and searchable at http://www.trumptwitterarchive.com/archive).

were wreaking destruction in the Capitol—that "we love you, you're very special."[160] To date, the President has taken no responsibility and shown no personal regret for his role in what occurred. This is clear evidence that the President acted willfully in inciting the mob.

Both members of the mob and Members of Congress recognized that it was the President who had sent the mob to Congress, they reasonably understood what he was saying,[161] and that it was he alone who could pull them back. A man inside the Capitol was captured on video saying: "Our president wants us here . . . We wait and take orders from our president."[162] Members of Congress, in turn, called on the President to call off his mob. As Representative Mike Gallagher tweeted during the Capitol occupation, "Mr. President. You have got to stop this. You are the only person who can call this off."[163] Similarly, Mick Mulvaney, the President's former Chief of Staff, tweeted, "The President's tweet is not enough. He can stop this now and needs to do exactly that. Tell these folks to go home."[164] But these pleas fell on deaf ears until well into the sacking of the Capitol. That further proves willful conduct.

Many others, including current and former members of President Trump's administration, have recognized that the President intended to incite violence aimed at the Capitol. As now former-Secretary of Education Betsy DeVos told the President, "[t]here is no mistaking the impact your rhetoric had on the situation."[165] Lawmakers similarly recognized the President's intent. As Senator Lisa Murkowski remarked, the President "told his supporters to fight. How are they supposed to take that? It's an order from the president. And so that's what they did. They came up and they fought and people were harmed, and injured and died."[166] Senator Mitt Romney echoed these sentiments: "What happened here today was an insurrection, incited by the President of the United States."[167] So did Senator Sasse: "This violence was the inevitable and ugly outcome of the president's addiction to constantly stoking division."[168] As Representative Liz Cheney noted

[160] Petras, et al. *Timeline: How a Trump mob stormed the US Capitol, forcing Washington into lockdown*, Yahoo News (Jan. 8, 2021).

[161] Michael Phillips and Jennifer Levitz, *One Trump Fan's Descent Into the U.S. Capitol Mob*, Wall Street Journal (Jan. 10, 2021). ("He said, 'Hey, I need my digital soliders to show up on January 6,' Mr. Sweet says of the President. 'And we all did.'").

[162] Dan Barry, et al., *'Our President Wants Us Here': The Mob That Stormed the Capitol*, N. Y. Times (Jan. 9, 2021); *see also* Amanda Seitz, *Mob at U.S. Capitol encouraged by online conspiracy theories*, AP (Jan. 7, 2021); Amy Brittain, et al., *The Capitol mob: A raging collection of grievances and disillusionment*, Wash. Post (Jan. 10, 2021)

[163] Editorial, *Mike Gallagher is right: 'Call it off, Mr. President'*, Wisconsin State Journal (Jan. 6, 2021).

[164] Mick Mulvaney (@MickMulvaney), Twitter (Jan. 6, 2021, 3:01 PM), https://twitter.com/MickMulvaney/status/1346909665423196162.

[165] Betsy Devos Letter of Resignation (Jan. 7, 2021) available at https://int.nyt.com/data/documenttools/devos-resignation/abedee707cb0984a/full.pdf.

[166] James Brooks, *Alaska Sen. Lisa Murkowski calls on President Trump to resign, questions her future as a Republican*, Anchorage Daily News (Jan. 9, 2021).

[167] *Today's Rampage at the Capitol, as It Happened*, N. Y. Times (Jan. 6, 2021).

[168] Michael Levenson, Steve Inskeep, *Ben Sasse Rips Trump For Stoking Mob, Calls Josh Hawley's Objection 'Really Dumbass'*, NPR (Jan. 8, 2021).

after President Trump told his mob to "get rid of" her: "There's no question the president formed the mob, the president incited the mob, the president addressed the mob. He lit the flame."[169] There is thus overwhelming evidence that President Trump committed the "high Crimes and Misdemeanors" charged in the article of impeachment against him.

3. President Trump's Conduct Harmed Core National Interests

President Trump's impeachable conduct, exacerbated by his further acts and omissions after he incited the crowd to attack the Capitol, grievously injured the national interests of the United States. It threatened democratic self-governance by interfering with the peaceful transition of power, imperiled a coequal branch of government, endangered our national security, and betrayed his oath of office and the trust of the American people.

a. Attack on Democratic Processes and the Peaceful Transition of Power

The insurrection incited by President Trump had a clear goal: attack, menace, obstruct, and ultimately prevent Congress in any way from carrying out its solemn constitutional duty to count the Electoral College vote. In fact, the rioters managed to delay the democratic processes for at least six hours. And, although the Joint Session reconvened and fulfilled its duty that same day, the lasting injury to our nation cannot be overstated.

At the heart of our Constitution is a commitment to popular sovereignty. At the core of that framework is the election of representatives to the United States Congress and the establishment of the Electoral College as the method of selection for the President and Vice President of the United States. The democratically elected Members of the Congress are charged with legislating and carrying important constitutional duties on behalf of the American people.

Under the Twelfth Amendment and the Electoral Count Act of 1887, the Congress is responsible for counting and the Electoral College votes, while the Vice President, as president of the Senate, plays a ministerial role in the proceedings.[170] In this way, the will of the American people is formally implemented, and the legitimacy to exercise the authorities of the national government bestowed on our elected federal officials. Another purpose of this process is to facilitate the orderly and peaceful transfer of power between elected officials.

The course of conduct President Trump pursued leading up to January 6, 2021 directly sought to undermine that very foundation of our Constitution. His conduct, contrary to our democracy, encouraged and foreseeably resulted in violent chaos aimed to subvert and obstruct the peaceful transfer of power. President Trump for weeks promoted not only false allegations of voter fraud, but the fringe constitutional theory that the Vice President is the sole arbiter of the Electoral College vote. The President then used the rage he had incited to encourage a physical assault on our the Capitol, in the very moments that the peaceful transfer of power administered by our elected officials was underway. In sum, the President's conduct in inciting an insurrection

---

[169] Justine Coleman, *Liz Cheney blames Trump for riots: 'He lit the flame'*, The Hill (Jan. 6, 2021).

[170] U.S. CONST. amend. XII.; Electoral Count Act of 1887, Pub. L. 49-90, 24 Stat. 373.

against our government, designed to subvert and obstruct the results of our free and fair elections, caused serious harm to our nation's fundamental interest in orderly democratic self-governance.

The Framers included the power of impeachment to thwart exactly such attempts at eroding our nation's commitment to popular sovereignty. As explained in the Judiciary Committee's previous impeachment report from the 116th Congress: *"[T]he true nature of this threat is its rejection of government by 'We the People,'* who would 'ordain and establish' the Constitution … When the President concludes that elections threaten his continued grasp on power, and therefore seeks to corrupt or interfere with them, he denies the very premise of our constitutional system. The American people choose their leaders; *a President who wields power to destroy opponents or manipulate elections is a President who rejects democracy itself."* [171]

b. Imperiling a Coordinate Branch

By engaging in this course of conduct President Trump willfully incited violence against the United States Congress, a coequal branch of the United States government, and the Vice President of the United States. Indeed, the violence that ensued jeopardized the safety of nearly the entire Legislative Branch, their staff, the many non-partisan workers employed by Congress, and the law enforcement officers serving to protect the Capitol. The insurrection incited by the President also threatened the safety of the three most senior officials in the presidential line of succession: Vice President Mike Pence, Speaker of the House Nancy Pelosi, and President pro tempore of the Senate Senator Chuck Grassley.

As described in detail in this report, many Members of Congress and their staff were forced to hide under tables or in offices while they awaited evacuation by law enforcement, while others were trapped on the House and Senate floor. Many feared for their lives, as armed attackers banged on the doors, and Capitol Police drew weapons.[172] Indeed, as set forth, at least five deaths occurred as a result of the violent mob's ambush on our government.

In short, the insurrectionists incited by President Trump threatened the lives of everyone who works at the U.S. Capitol, including officials in the presidential line of succession, as well as the continued existence of a functioning Legislative Branch. As Representative Sean Maloney, who was present in the Capitol when the mob violence occurred, cautioned: "[f]or those pretending it's something less than a violent insurrection, please watch and wake up. This is what [President Trump] and his enablers incited. He must be removed and held accountable."[173]

---

[171] See H. Rept. 116-346 at 53. (emphasis added).

[172] *See e.g.* Tasneem Nashrulla, Members Of Congress Described What It Was Like When A Pro-Trump Mob Stormed The Capitol, Buzzfeed (Jan. 6, 2021).

[173] Jon Swaine, Dalton Bennett, Joyce Sohyun Lee & Meg Kelly, Video shows fatal shooting of Ashli Babbitt in the Capitol, WashPo (Jan. 8, 2021); Sean Patrick Maloney (@RepSeanMaloney), Twitter (Jan. 8, 2021 2:28 PM), https://twitter.com/repseanmaloney/status/1347626297367941121?s=27.

c. *Harm to Our Nation's National Security*

President Trump's conduct directly harmed the national security of the United States. In the most immediate sense, the President's incitement of the mob assault on the Capitol may have exposed sensitive materials and locations to the public creating immediate national security risks. In the long term, the insurrection caused lasting damage to the nation's international reputation as a bastion of democratic order, undermining American "soft power" and emboldening our adversaries abroad.

Although there is not yet a complete account of the immediate consequences of the insurrection to our national security, the insurrectionists had access to, and stole, sensitive materials and electronics. As Michael Sherwin, acting United States attorney for the District of Columbia explained, "electronic items, were stolen from senators' offices. Documents, materials, were stolen, and we have to identify what was done, mitigate that, and it could have potential national security equities. If there was damage, we don't know the extent of that yet."[174] Further, insurrectionists posted photos of areas in the Capitol generally off limits to the public, and some even livestreamed the attack on the internet. Both the Senate and the House, in coordination with federal law enforcement officials, will have to conduct an arduous top-to-bottom review to determine what devices have been stolen, whether documents have been taken or copied, and even if listening devices have been left behind by rioters.[175]

In addition to this immediate damage, the insurrection incited by President Trump has likely done incalculable damage to the United States' reputation abroad as an exemplar of democratic self-governance. This event was broadcast live, in real time. Accordingly, it threatens to undermine the U.S.'s moral authority and hamper our ability to persuade other countries to take actions beneficial to U.S. national interests in the future. It will take substantial public diplomacy work by future Presidents to overcome the international damage done to the prestige of the United States. As reported in the news, for America's adversaries, "there was no greater proof of the fallibility of Western democracy than the sight of the U.S. Capitol shrouded in smoke and besieged by a mob whipped up by their unwillingly outgoing president."[176]

Already the insurrection incited by President Trump has been a propaganda boon to many authoritarian regimes. The Supreme Leader Ayatollah Khamenei of Iran said in a live televised speech that "[y]ou are now seeing the situation in the U.S. . . . . This is their democracy and human rights, this is their election scandal, these are their values. These values are being mocked by the whole world. Even their friends are laughing at them."[177] The foreign ministry of the People's Republic of China made public statements justifying that government's violent crackdown on

---

[174] Brian Fung, *Capitol riots raise urgent concerns about Congress's information security*, CNN (Jan. 8, 2021).

[175] Natasha Bertrand, *Justice Department warns of national security fallout from Capitol Hill insurrection*, POLITICO (Jan. 7, 2021).

[176] Alexander Smith & Saphora Smith, *U.S. foes like China and Iran see opportunity in the chaos of Trump-stoked riot at Capitol*, NBC News, (Jan. 8, 2021).

[177] *Id.*

Hong Kong pro-democracy protestors through comparisons to the rioters that attacked the U.S. Capitol.[178] And the President of Zimbabwe tweeted a call for the U.S. to end economic sanctions against that country's authoritarian regime stating that "President Trump extended painful economic sanctions placed on Zimbabwe, citing concerns about Zimbabwe's democracy" but that the mob attack on the U.S. Capitol "showed that the U.S. has no moral right to punish another nation under the guise of upholding democracy."[179]

d. Betrayal of Oath of Office and of the American People's Trust

President Trump's incitement of the attack on the Capitol served only his interests. The President lost the election and—when he could not convince the courts or other elected officials to override—he engaged in disinformation and demagoguery to incite a mob in a last-ditch effort to retain power.

In other words, President Trump compromised our national security, the foundation of our democratic system, and our nation's elected leaders, all in pursuit of his own personal and political advantage and self-interest. Through this conduct President Trump abdicated his Constitutional oath to faithfully execute our laws and his duty to place our nation's interest, above his own. As President Trump's former National Security Advisor H.R. McMaster characterized it: "It was, in every sense of the phrase, a dereliction of duty."[180] Following the conduct that led to his impeachment in December 2019, President Trump, for all the country and all the world to see, has once again demonstrated that he is unfit for office and will use any official means at his disposal— regardless of the harm caused to our nation—to hold onto political power.

C. The Irrelevance of the Criminal Code and the *Brandenburg* Test

It may well be the case that President Trump's conduct on January 6, 2021—and other actions that he took in seeking to overturn and subvert the certification of the election results— violated the federal criminal code. Ultimately, that is a judgment for prosecutors and courts to make. The only question here is whether President Trump's conduct warrants impeachment. As the House Judiciary Committee has previously explained, "[o]ffenses against the Constitution are different in kind than offenses against the criminal code . . . Impeachment and criminality must therefore be assessed separately."[181] Accordingly, though it may indeed have done so, President

---

[178] *Id.*; *What Are Asian Governments Saying About the Storming of the US Capitol?*, The Diplomat (Jan. 8, 2021); Foreign Ministry Spokesperson Hua Chunying's Regular Press Conference on January 7, 2021, Ministry of Foreign Affairs of the People's Republic of China (Jan. 7, 2021)

[179] President of Zimbabwe (@edmnangagwa), Twitter (Jan. 7, 2021, 8:42 AM), https://twitter.com/edmnangagwa/status/1347176848694931457.

[180] H.R. McMaster (@LTGHRMcMaster), Twitter (Jan. 7, 2021, 3:05 PM), https://twitter.com/LTGHRMcMaster/status/1347273185641734144 ("The reasons for yesterday's criminal assault on our Congress and election process are many. But foremost among them is the sad reality that President Trump and other officials have repeatedly compromised our principles in pursuit of partisan advantage and personal gain. Those who engaged in disinformation and demagoguery in pursuit of self-interest abdicated their responsibility to the American people. It was, in every sense of the phrase, a dereliction of duty").

[181] *See* H. Rept. 116-346 at 56.

Trump's conduct need not have violated any federal criminal statutes in order for them to constitute "high Crimes and Misdemeanors" under the Constitution.

Nor is the Supreme Court's decision in *Brandenburg v. Ohio* relevant to the question of impeachment.[182] In *Brandenburg*, the Court clarified that the First Amendment allows the criminal punishment of incitement. It then limited such liability to cases where "advocacy is directed to inciting or producing imminent lawless action and is likely to incite or produce such action."[183]

To apply *Brandenburg* here—and to insist that President Trump cannot be impeached unless the *Brandenburg* test is met—would be to commit two fatal category errors.[184]

The first error involves a misstatement of First Amendment law. The Free Speech Clause guarantees that private citizens can engage in certain forms of expression without government regulation or prohibition. But it applies very differently to speech by government officials and public employees. By virtue of his high office, President Trump is no ordinary citizen. He occupies a position of public trust and directs the operations of the Executive Branch. As a high-level public official, the President is subject to different rules than private citizens and can be held accountable for his expression (including all expression relating to his office) in ways that they cannot be. That is a basic and well-established precept of First Amendment law. In fact, as Professor Ilya Somin observed, "Donald Trump himself has fired numerous cabinet officials and other subordinates because they expressed views he didn't like."[185]

The second and more fundamental error involves a misunderstanding of the Impeachment Clause. For many of the same reasons that impeachment does not necessarily turn on criminality, it is not governed by a standard that defines when a person can be held responsible civilly or criminally for their speech. Impeachment is about preserving the Nation from a threat to the constitutional order, not imposing punishment. Nowhere did the Framers suggest that a President must be allowed to remain in office if his abuses involved speech that would otherwise be shielded from criminal regulation by the First Amendment. This would be a strange and irrational limitation: Presidents would be free to openly advocate the overthrow of the United States government, or the adoption of fascism, and Congress would be powerless to remove them on that basis. Moreover, given that many prior impeachable offenses have involved at least some conduct that might rank as protected speech, applying a rigid First Amendment rule in this field would risk obfuscating Presidential conduct—whether involving speech or not—that menaces the American democratic system.[186]

---

[182] 395 U.S. 444 (1969).

[183] *Id.* at 447.

[184] Constitutional scholars have recently elaborated on these category errors. *See, e.g.*, Jonathan H. Adler, *Yes, Congress May Impeach and Remove President Trump for Inciting Lawless Behavior at the Capitol*, The Volokh Conspiracy (January 8, 2021); Ilya Somin, *The First Amendment Doesn't Protect Trump Against Impeachment for his Role in Inciting the Assault on the Capitol*, The Volokh Conspiracy (January 8, 2021).

[185] *See id.*

[186] H. Mis. Doc. No. 42, 40th Cong. (1868); H.Res.755, 116th Cong. (2019).

Simply put, President Trump has no free speech defense. President Trump is not a private citizen, free to say whatever he wants without accepting the consequences or recognizing the effects it might have on our system of government. As the head of the Executive Branch, his words can shake the nation—and so he is held to a higher standard than private citizens. Moreover, when it comes to the impeachment power, the question is not whether the President was free to say what he said. It is whether he has engaged in conduct that threatens the constitutional order. President Nixon engaged in speech when he ordered the cover-up of his crimes. President Trump engaged in speech when he sought to extort President Zelensky of Ukraine. Federal judges have engaged in speech when they abused their position. Yet neither the House nor the Senate have ever suggested that just because an impeachable offense involved speech, it cannot support impeachment unless some First Amendment standard is met.

Accordingly, the judgment for Congress to make is not whether President Trump had a free speech right to say what he said on January 6, 2021. It is whether that conduct qualified as a high Crime and Misdemeanor under the applicable constitutional standard. For the reasons set forth above, there can be no doubt that it did: inciting a mob to assault the Capitol while Congress meets in Joint Session to count the electoral votes in the presidential election results is plainly an impeachable offense.

III.   The Need for Immediate Consideration of Impeachment

President Trump's behavior requires immediate congressional action.

First, President Trump poses an imminent threat to the safety and security of the United States. His continued presence in office is a clear and present danger to the United States. He has interfered with the peaceful transition of power and his actions show that he will continue to do so unless removed. He incited a mob to violence in order to try to overturn an election he lost and to disrupt the Joint Session of Congress that would confirm the result. President Trump not only failed to stop his supporters from invading the Capitol, he encouraged and supported their efforts. As Congress came under threat, his responsibility was to turn the mob away. But did not instruct supporters to call off their attack. Instead, as a sworn federal law officer lay injured and dying, and government officials raced to protect themselves from the armed mob, President Trump continued his attacks on Vice President Pence for failing to overturn the election results, spread false claims that he had won the election, called Members of Congress to lobby them to continue to object to the counting of electors in States won by President-elect Biden, and reassured the insurrectionists that they were "loved."

Since then, instead of expressing remorse about his conduct, he continues to deny responsibility for the consequences of his actions, justifying the mob's behavior through his false claims of election fraud. Recent events may well have emboldened President Trump's supporters to continue their efforts to disrupt the transfer of power before or on January 20, 2021. The risk that President Trump will once again support this disruption to the peril of our security and democracy is too great to leave him in office for the remaining days of his term.

Second, it is equally important that Congress send a clear message and establish a precedent that the President's conduct subjects him to impeachment and removal from office. That message may not be well received by President Trump and his supporters, but Congress has an obligation to warn future presidents that conduct of this nature is incompatible with the Office of the Presidency. This message must be sent even on the President's last day in office. There is no merit to the startling and dangerous idea that a president may engage in high Crimes and Misdemeanors in their final weeks in office and escape the operation of the Impeachment Clause. President Trump incited an insurrection to try to break the Constitutional order, overturn an election, and prevent the ratification of a new President elected by the people in a free and fair election. In these circumstances, he has left the House of Representatives no choice.

A. Imminent Threat to the United States

President Trump's impeachable offense of incitement—as well as his conduct leading up to and his subsequent acts and omissions during the mob's unlawful entry into the Capitol—demonstrate why he cannot be permitted to remain in office. President Trump failed to defend the Capitol. His conduct on January 6th and afterwards gives no reason to hope that he will adequately oversee the necessary preparations and security for the inauguration of President-elect Biden on January 20, 2021, and instead suggests the opposite. Moreover, his actions on January 6th are consistent with a long pattern of behavior where President Trump has tried to stir up lawless extremism, overturn the results of the election, and obstruct the lawful certification of electors.

1. President Trump Failed to Protect the Capitol, the Vice President, and Members of Congress During the Joint Session of Congress

Although President Trump did not literally march to the Capitol with his supporters after his speech on January 6th as he said he would, his instructions and intentions guided the crowd that day as surely as if he were at the head of the mob he orchestrated. His supporters thought they were doing President Trump's bidding by seeking to disrupt the Joint Session of Congress that would declare that President-elect Biden won the election. In fact, they directly said so on social media, in live videos, and when interviewed by the police following arrests.

As President Trump's supporters attacked the Capitol, the President did nothing. At 1:00 PM on January 6th, as required by the 12th Amendment and the Electoral Count Act, Congress met in Joint Session to count the electoral votes.[187] By 1:22 PM, Capitol Police had already begun issuing emergency evacuation orders.[188] The crowd that had gathered to watch President Trump's speech walked to the Capitol, and had begun to breach the security barriers surrounding the

---

[187] Domenico Montanaro, *Timeline: How One Of The Darkest Days In American History Unfolded*, NPR (Jan. 7, 2021)

[188] Chris Marquette et al., *Pro-Trump protesters storm Capitol during Electoral College certification, causing lockdown*, Roll Call (Jan. 6, 2021) (At 1:22 PM Capitol Police ordered the evacuation of the Cannon House Office Building and at 1:47 PM the department announced the evacuation was all clear. However, by 2:03 PM Capitol Police issued its relocation order for Cannon House Office Building and by 2:18 PM Capitol Police had issued its lockdown of the Capitol complex)

Capitol. President Trump watched the mob of his supporters attack the Capitol on television as they occurred.[189]

Instead of acting to stop the riot, however, President Trump continued to criticize those officials he viewed as not sufficiently supportive. He disparaged Vice President Pence, who refused to overturn the election, rightly recognizing that he did not have the authority to do so under the Constitution.[190] At 1:49 PM—while the Capitol was under siege—President Trump tweeted a video of the rally.[191] In the speech that he retweeted, he told the same crowd that was now storming the Capitol that "our country has had enough. We will not take it anymore and that's what this is all about. And to use a favorite term that all of you people really came up with, we will stop the steal. . . . you'll never take back our country with weakness. You have to show strength, and you have to be strong."[192] In other words, just as his supporters were beginning to act, President Trump tweeted the very speech encouraging them to "be strong" and repeating the debunked lies about the election.

By 2:20 PM, the entire country saw on live television that the mob had caused both the House and the Senate to adjourn.[193] Yet at 2:24 p.m., President Trump tweeted his anger about Vice President Pence: "Mike Pence didn't have the courage to do what should have been done to protect our Country and our Constitution, giving States a chance to certify a corrected set of facts, not the fraudulent or inaccurate ones which they were asked to previously certify. USA demands the truth!"[194] These statements occurred while the Capitol was under siege, insurrectionists roamed its halls, and Members of Congress huddled to protect themselves from the intruders.

President Trump—watching the violence unfold on television and his mob of supporters disrupt the proceedings—was "borderline enthusiastic because it meant the certification was being derailed."[195] His reaction "genuinely freaked people out"[196] and he "repeatedly refused requests to get him to say something clearly rejecting the violence."[197] Although he tweeted twice in the mid-afternoon asking the crowd to be "peaceful," these statements were not sufficient and were overshadowed by his other words. He told them to "stay" peaceful although he could clearly see

---

[189] Maggie Haberman, *Trump Told Crowd, "You Will Never Take Back Our Country with Weakness.* N. Y. Times (Jan. 6, 2021).

[190] *Id.*

[191] Donald J. Trump (@realDonaldTrump), Twitter (Jan. 6, 2021, 1:49 PM) (online and searchable at http://www.trumptwitterarchive.com/archive).

[192] Julia Jacobo, *This is what Trump told supporters before many stormed Capitol Hill*, ABC News (Jan. 7, 2021).

[193] Shelly Tan et al., *How one of America's ugliest days unraveled inside and outside the Capitol*, Wash. Post (Jan. 9, 2021).

[194] Donald J. Trump (@realDonaldTrump), Twitter (Jan. 6, 2021, 2:24 PM) (online and searchable at http://www.trumptwitterarchive.com/archive).

[195] Kaitlan Collins (@kaitlancollins), Twitter (Jan. 6, 2021, 10:34 PM), https://twitter.com/kaitlancollins/status/1347023890959228933.

[196] *Id.*

[197] Maggie Haberman (@maggieNYT), Twitter (Jan. 6, 2021, 11:19 PM), https://twitter.com/mknz/status/1347036422360813571.

they were anything but peaceful. Indeed, in a video issued at 4:17 PM, President Trump opened by telling the mob, "I know your pain. I know you're hurt. We had an election that was stolen from us," and then told them, "We love you, you're very special."[198] And at 6:01 PM, President Trump appeared to justify and celebrate the day's events: "These are the things and events that happen when a sacred landslide election victory is so unceremoniously & viciously stripped away from great patriots who have been badly & unfairly treated for so long."[199] He concluded, "*Remember this day forever!*"[200]

During the attack, Vice President Pence, Members of Congress, and staff were sheltering in secure locations. Spurred by the false claims of fraud, some of the attackers said, "Tell Pelosi we're coming for that [expletive]," and "Hang Mike Pence."[201] Some attackers carried zip ties intended to be used as handcuffs.[202] A noose was hung outside the Capitol.[203] Multiple members of the Capitol Police were severely injured or killed.[204]

President Trump, however, was not focused on the security or well-being of those under siege. Instead, he was continuing to try to overturn the election and calling Senators to object to Biden electors. Immediately after the Senators had been evacuated from the Senate floor, President Trump called Senator Mike Lee—apparently trying to reach Senator Tommy Tuberville.[205] Senator Lee handed his phone to Senator Tuberville and the President asked him to make more objections to the Electoral College vote.[206] And later that night, President Trump's lawyer Rudy Giuliani tried to take advantage of the chaos by following up on President Trump's call. He left a message with Senator Tuberville to continue to object "so that we get ourselves into tomorrow."[207] In short, President Trump's focus during and after the attack that day was not on trying to protect the safety or security of the Capitol. Instead, he was trying illegitimately to derail the Joint Session that would officially count the Electoral College votes confirming President-elect Biden's victory.

---

[198] Petras et al., *Timeline: How a Trump mob stormed the US Capitol, forcing Washington into lockdown*, Yahoo News (Jan. 8, 2021).

[199] Donald J. Trump (@realDonaldTrump), Twitter (Jan. 6, 2021, 6:01 PM) (online and searchable at http://www.trumptwitterarchive.com/archive).

[200] *Id.* (emphasis added),

[201] Matthew S. Schwartz, *As Inauguration Nears, Concern Of More Violence Grows*, NPR (Jan. 9, 2021).

[202] Devlin Barrett et al., *FBI focuses on whether some Capitol rioters intended to harm lawmakers or take hostages*, Wash. Post (Jan.8, 2021).

[203] Rebecca Shabad, *Noose appears near Capitol; protesters seen carrying Confederate flags*, NBC News (Jan. 6, 2021).

[204] Peter Hermann & Julia Zauzmer, *Beaten, sprayed with mace and hit with stun guns: police describe injuries to dozens of officers during assault on U.S. Capitol*, Wash. Post (Jan. 11, 2021); Evan Hill et al., 'They Got a Officer!': How a Mob Dragged and Beat Police at the Capitol (N. Y. Times Jan. 11, 2021); *Loss of USCP Officer Brian D. Sicknick*, United States Capitol Police Press Release (Jan. 7, 2021).

[205] Sunlen Serfaty et al., *As riot raged at Capitol, Trump tried to call senators to overturn election*, CNN (Jan. 8, 2021).

[206] *Id.*

[207] *Id.*

Finally, the threat of violence has not subsided. Some of President Trump's supporters have said they will return to Washington, D.C. prior to the Inauguration to foment violence: "Many of Us will return on January 19, 2021, carrying Our weapons, in support of Our nation's resolve, to which [sic] the world will never forget!!!"[208] Other reports suggest a proposed second attack on January 17th, along with attacks on state capitols.[209] Federal law enforcement has warned that armed protests are being planned in state capitols in the days leading up to and on Inauguration Day, with groups planning to "storm" government offices.[210] Additionally, Capitol Police have been reported to have briefed lawmakers of three more potential protests at the Capitol in coming days, including one which would involve "insurrectionists forming a perimeter around the Capitol, the White House and the Supreme Court, and then blocking Democrats from entering the Capitol — perhaps even killing them — so that Republicans could take control of the government."[211]

President Trump has demonstrated that he is unfit to lead and is a danger to the Nation. Instead of trying to stop these attacks, he incited them. Instead of defending the Capitol, he encouraged the breach of its barricades. Instead of condemning the insurrectionists, he praised them. Accordingly, our country can take no chances in the remaining days of President Trump's Presidency.

2. President Trump Has Demonstrated No Remorse Since January 6th

Since the attack on the Capitol, the President has shown no remorse for his role in inciting the violence. President Trump has failed to make any public statement that unambiguously condemns the actions of his supporters in attacking the Capitol—and he has utterly refused to acknowledge his own role in fomenting the insurrection. Instead, insisting to reporters that his speech prior to the insurrection was "totally appropriate."[212]

Far from it. President Trump's statements since the events of January 6th have only fanned the flames. That night, after law enforcement had succeeded in clearing many of the attackers, the President excused and even *celebrated* their criminal actions, declaring them "great patriots" who had "been badly & unfairly treated for so long," and urging them to "Remember this day forever!"[213] Because this incendiary statement violated Twitter's standards, the President's tweet was first flagged and later removed by Twitter, and the President was initially suspended from

---

[208]Matthew S. Schwartz, *As Inauguration Nears, Concern Of More Violence Grows*, NPR (Jan. 9, 2021).

[209] Devlin Barrett et al., FBI focuses on whether some Capitol rioters intended to harm lawmakers or take hostages, Wash. Post (Jan.8, 2021).

[210] Aaron Katersky & Celia Darrough, *Armed protests being planned at all 50 state capitols, FBI bulletin says*, ABC News (Jan. 11, 2021).

[211] Matt Fuller, House Democrats Briefed On 3 Terrifying Plots To Overthrow Government, Huff Post (Jan. 12, 2021).

[212] Kevin Liptak & Betsy Klein, *Defiant Trump denounces violence but takes no responsibility for inciting deadly riot,* CNN (Jan. 12, 2021).

[213] Donald J. Trump (@realDonaldTrump), Twitter (Jan. 6, 2021, 6:01 PM) (online and searchable at http://www.trumptwitterarchive.com/archive).

using his Twitter account for 12 hours,[214] "due to the risk of further incitement of violence."[215] Similarly, YouTube, Instagram, and Facebook, within 24 hours, removed from their platforms a similarly inflammatory video the President had released earlier that day. Facebook justified its removal of the video because of its conclusion that the President's words on balance "contribute[d] to rather than diminishe[d] the risk of ongoing violence"[216]

On January 7, despite pleas from advisers and allies to address the horrified nation, President Trump remained publicly silent throughout the day—failing to take responsibility for his actions or to take any step to salve the wounds suffered by the nation and government that he had sworn an oath to serve.[217] That evening, the President finally addressed the nation in a prerecorded, scripted video. Although the President's recorded remarks belatedly acknowledged that "demonstrators who infiltrated the Capitol" had "defiled the seat of American democracy," he failed to rebuke his supporters for attacking the halls of Congress in his name.[218] Most importantly, the President expressed no remorse for—and did not even acknowledge—his own central role in inciting the attackers to desecrate the seat of American government and endanger the lives of thousands of men and women, including Capitol Police and other law enforcement, Members of Congress, Capitol and congressional staff, and many others working in service of the American government on January 6, 2021.[219]

In the ensuing days, the President's absence of remorse became even more stark. Instead of working to repair the damage he had caused, he added yet more fuel to the anti-democratic fire his past conduct had ignited. On January 8th, the President tweeted: "The 75,000,000 great American Patriots who voted for me, AMERICA FIRST, and MAKE AMERICA GREAT AGAIN, will have a GIANT VOICE long into the future. They will not be disrespected or treated unfairly in any way, shape or form!!!"[220] That same day, the President announced by tweet that he would "not be going to the Inauguration on January 20th" to observe the sacred American tradition of the peaceful transfer of power from one President to the next.[221]

Later that day, the President used the White House's official @POTUS account to tweet yet more inflammatory material, falsely asserting that "Twitter employees have coordinated with

---

[214] Mike Snider, *President Trump deletes tweets after Twitter, Facebook and Instagram lock down accounts for 'violations'*, USA Today (Jan. 6, 2021).

[215] Twitter Safety (@TwitterSafety), Twitter (Jan. 8, 2021, 6:21PM), https://twitter.com/TwitterSafety/status/1347684877634838528.

[216] *Our Response to the Violence in Washington*, Facebook (Jan. 6, 2021).

[217] *See* Philip Rucker et al, *After inciting mob attack, Trump retreats in rage. Then, grudgingly, he admits his loss*, Wash. Post (Jan. 7, 2021).

[218] Donald J. Trump (@realDonaldTrump), Twitter (Jan. 7, 2021, 7:10 PM) (online and searchable at http://www.trumptwitterarchive.com/archive).

[219] To the contrary, the President told yet more lies, falsely stating that he had "immediately deployed the National Guard and federal law enforcement to secure the building and expel the intruders"—when in fact President Trump took *no action* to protect the Capitol or those inside it.

[220] Donald J. Trump (@realDonaldTrump), Twitter, (Jan. 8, 2021, 9:46 AM) (online and searchable at http://www.trumptwitterarchive.com/archive)

[221] *Id.* at (Jan. 8, 2021, 10:44 AM).

the Democrats and the Radical Left in removing my account from their platform, to silence me—and YOU, the 75,000,000 great . . . patriots who voted for me" and threatening: "We will not be SILENCED!"[222] To this day, the President refuses to acknowledge or express any hint of personal remorse for his role in the January 6th insurrection, instead publicly claiming no responsibility[223].

In stark contrast to the President, Republican Members of Congress and those in the Administration have widely recognized and expressed horror at the attack on the Capitol and the President's role in inciting it. Immediately upon returning to their respective chambers after the attackers had been forcibly removed, members of the President's own party in the House and Senate recognized that "what happened here today was an insurrection, incited by the President of the United States."[224] In public statements on the floor of Congress and elsewhere, the President's fellow Republicans made clear: "There's no question the president formed the mob. The President incited the mob. The President addressed the mob. He lit the flame."[225] They declared that the attack on the Capitol was "the inevitable and ugly outcome of the President's addiction to constantly stoking division," and the President's conduct "was a flagrant dereliction of his duty to uphold and defend the Constitution."[226]

Beginning the next day, a series of members of the President's Administration resigned in protest of his role in the attack. Secretary of Education DeVos resigned her Cabinet post due to the "unconscionable" attack, and observed in her resignation letter to President Trump: "There is no mistaking the impact your rhetoric had on the situation."[227] Secretary of Transportation Elaine Chao likewise resigned from the Cabinet,[228] and Special Envoy Mulvaney, previously President Trump's Acting Chief of Staff, resigned as well, declaring "I can't do it. I can't stay."[229] Numerous

---

[222] *Id; See also Salvador Rodriguez, Trump tweets from POTUS handle account, says looking 'at the possibilities of building out our own platform', CNBC (Jan. 8, 2021).*

[223] Kevin Liptak & Betsy Klein, *Defiant Trump denounces violence but takes no responsibility for inciting deadly riot, CNN (Jan. 12, 2021).*

[224] *Romney Condemns Insurrection at U.S. Capitol, Senator Mitt Romney: Press Releases (Jan. 6, 2021). see also, e.g., Oma Seddiq, Sen. Lindsey Graham blames Trump for Capitol riots and says the president needs to 'understand that his actions were the problem', Business Insider (Jan. 7, 2021) ("When it comes to accountability, the president needs to understand that his actions were the problem, not the solution."); Malachi Barrett, Michigan representatives denounce attack on U.S. Capitol by pro-Trump mob, MLive (Jan. 6, 2021). (decrying "attempt to overthrow the workings of the U.S. government, the legislative branch," and urging President Trump "to not just strongly condemn the violence, not just tell people go home, but also recognize and acknowledge Biden as president-elect").*

[225] Statement of Rep. Cheney, available at https://www.nytimes.com/2021/01/06/us/politics/trump-speech-capitol.html.

[226] Statement of Sen. Sasse, available at https://www.npr.org/sections/congress-electoral-college-tally-live-updates/2021/01/08/954854250/gop-sen-sasse-rips-trump-for-stoking-mob-calls-hawleys-objection-really-dumbass.

[227] Betsy Devos Letter of Resignation (Jan. 7, 2021) (Available at https://www.washingtonpost.com/context/betsy-devos-resignation-letter/cfd93504-2353-4ac3-8e71-155446242dda/.).

[228] Kevin Liptak et al., *Some Trump administration officials resign while others stay to prevent chaos, CNN (Jan. 7, 2021).*

[229] Erin Schumaker, *Trump officials who have resigned in the wake of attack on Capitol, ABC News (Jan. 9, 2021).*

other White House officials, too, tendered their resignations.[230] Additionally, former Acting Secretary of the Department of Homeland Security Chad Wolf "implore[d] the President" to "strongly condemn the violence that took place."[231]

Former Trump Administration officials have likewise rebuked the President and expressed horror at what his conduct has wrought. Attorney General Barr, accused the President of a "betrayal of his office," and declared that "orchestrating a mob to pressure Congress is inexcusable."[232] The President's former Secretary of Defense James Mattis declared that "[t]oday's violent assault on our Capitol, an effort to subjugate American democracy by mob rule, was fomented by Mr. Trump."[233] Former White House Chief of Staff John Kelly stated that "[w]hat happened on Capitol Hill ... is a direct result of [President Trump's] poisoning the minds of people with the lies and the fraud."[234] And former Speaker of the House John Boehner declared that "[t]he invasion of our Capitol by a mob, incited by lies from some entrusted with power, is a disgrace to all who sacrificed to build our Republic."[235]

Despite repeated entreaties, it took until January 10th for President Trump to order the flag of the United States to be flown at half-staff to commemorate the January 7th death of the Capitol Police officer who was murdered by the insurrectionists.[236] In contrast, the flag over the U.S. Capitol was lowered shortly after his death was confirmed.

The President's fellow Republicans recognize what he will not: his words incited a violent attack on the Capitol and the Congress. He "incited the mob" and "lit the flame," in the words of Congresswoman Cheney. Because the President has not repudiated the violent and unlawful actions of his followers or guided them to refrain from future antidemocratic attacks, he cannot be trusted to deter future violence or to remain in office.

---

[230] As of January 9, 2021, the list of individuals resigning from the White House includes John Costello, deputy assistant secretary for intelligence and security in the Commerce Department; Matthew Pottinger, White House deputy national security adviser; Sarah Matthews, White House deputy press secretary; Rickie Niceta, White House social secretary; and Stephanie Grisham, chief of staff to First Lady Melania Trump. *Id.*

[231] *Acting Secretary Wolf Condemns Violence at The U.S. Capitol, Dept. of Homeland Security* (Jan. 7, 2021). Former Acting Secretary Wolf resigned on Jan. 11, 2021, citing "court rulings regarding the validity of [his] authority as Acting Secretary" as the reason. *See* Priscilla Alvarez & Geneva Sands, A*cting Secretary of Homeland Security Chad Wolf resigns; FEMA Administrator Pete Gaynor to take over*, CNN (Jan. 11, 2021).

[232] Quint Forgey, *Barr: Trump committed 'betrayal of his office'*, Politico (Jan. 7, 2021).

[233] Amanda Macias, *Mattis blames Trump for violence at Capitol, says his actions 'poison our respect for fellow citizens'*, CNBC (Jan. 6, 2021).

[234]Christine Mui, *Ex-Trump Chief of Staff John Kelly supports 25th Amendment to remove president*, Boston Globe (Jan. 7, 2021).

[235] Scott Wartman, *Boehner: 'The GOP must awaken.' Former Speaker of the House slams the Republican Party over 'nightmare.'*, Cincinnati Enquirer (Jan. 7, 2021).

[236] David Choi, *Trump lowers the White House flag after pressure from both Republicans and Democrats*, Business Insider, (Jan. 11, 2021).

3. President Trump's Actions Are Consistent with His Past Pattern of Undermining the Public Peace and the Orderly Operation of Democracy

The Article of Impeachment charges President Trump for conduct connected to the events of January 6, 2021. The conduct that gives rise to that Article is, however, consistent with previous related conduct by President Trump that demonstrates an indifference to the public peace and to the lawful and orderly operation of our democratic government. That conduct encompasses his encouragement of lawless mob violence by his political supporters, and his urging of official actors to take ultra vires action to advance his falsehoods that he won the election and that it was stolen from him. The latter conduct includes a telephone call on January 2, 2021 in which he sought to induce the Secretary of State of Georgia to change the certified outcome of the 2020 presidential election in his favor. That President Trump has used the weight of his office to engage in such conduct in the past, and the recent escalation of that conduct which resulted in the January 6, 2021 insurrection, gives rise to a significant concern that, if not removed from office, President Trump will continue to engage in similar efforts to incite mass, violent lawless action during the remainder of his term.

President Trump has previously expressed both tacit and explicit support for mob violence perpetrated by his sympathizers. On August 12, 2017 multiple violent clashes broke out during the Unite the Right rally in Charlottesville, Virginia, including an incident in which one protester, a self-identified white supremacist, intentionally drove his car into a crowd of counter-protesters, killing one and injuring 19 others.[237] The violence perpetrated by the protesters, who celebrated white supremacy and included separatists who espouse civil war, drew nearly universal and immediate condemnation. Uniquely among prominent public officials, President Trump's statements condemned the hatred and violence "on many sides, on many sides" while also praising "very fine people on both sides."[238] In a context in which the values of human equality are enshrined in our Constitution and are universally agreed to be fundamental American values, all those who hold a position of trust under the Constitutional are expected to, and most regularly and loudly do, denounce white supremacy in clear and unambiguous terms. Against that backdrop, President Trump drew an equivalence between those who stood for white supremacy and those who stood against it. That public approach appears to convey a lack of disapprobation for the ideals and militant aspirations of the white supremacist movement, and was broadly so understood, including by prominent members of that movement.

During the 2020 Presidential campaign, President Trump was asked in the first Presidential Debate on September 29, 2020 to condemn white supremacists, but he would not. Asked by the debate moderator to condemn white supremacists and militia groups, and specifically prompted by the opposing candidate to denounce the group known as the Proud Boys, President Trump declined to denounce the group and instead issued a directive to them, stating, "Proud Boys, stand

---

[237] Jason Hanna et al., *Virginia governor to white nationalists: 'Go home … shame on you'*, CNN (Aug. 13, 2017).

[238] Glenn Thrush and Maggie Haberman, *Trump Gives White Supremacists an Unequivocal Boost*, N. Y. Times (Aug. 15, 2017).

back and stand by." On December 12, 2020—less than a month before the attack on the Capitol—a leader of the Proud Boys visited the White House.[239]

His disregard for lawful process and the orderly operation of government continued in the aftermath of the election, including during President Trump's January 2, 2021 call with Georgia state officials.[240] After Election Day, the state of Georgia's county canvass results showed that President Trump lost the election in Georgia by approximately 14,000 votes.[241] Much of the tally was conducted by automated tallying machines. Secretary Raffensperger then ordered a Risk Limiting Audit of the results, and directed that every county conduct a manual recount of the ballots to check the accuracy of the electronic tallying results. The audit resulted in a variance of 0.0099% in the vote differential between the candidates, which did not change the outcome. In the course of the audit, the state also discovered a number of ballots in two counties that had not been included in the original canvass.[242] After the audit and the inclusion of the missing ballots, the tally showed that President Trump had lost Georgia by more than 12,000 votes. As permitted by Georgia law, the Trump campaign requested a recount.[243]

Under Georgia law, the Secretary of State was required to certify the results of the election on November 20, 2020, and the Governor of the state was then required to promptly certify the appointment of a slate of presidential electors in accordance with the election results. President Trump publicly exhorted both men not to do so. Secretary Raffensperger nevertheless proceeded to certify the results on November 20, 2020, and Georgia Governor Kemp duly certified the appointment of a slate of electors that same day.[244] The Trump campaign's recount request, which proceeded in parallel, was performed electronically pursuant to state law.[245] After the recount, the vote count remained materially unchanged; Georgia recertified the election result on December 7, 2020.[246]

[239] David Smith et al., *Donald Trump refuses to condemn white supremacists at presidential debate*, The Guardian (Sep. 29, 2020); Craig Timberg & Drew Harwell, *Pro-Trump forums erupt with violent threats ahead of Wednesday's rally against the 2020 election*, Wash. Post (Jan. 5, 2021).

[240] Amy Gardner & Paulina Firozi, *Here's the full transcript and audio of the call between Trump and Raffensperger*, Wash. Post (Jan. 5, 2021).

[241] Christina A. Cassidy, *EXPLAINER: Is Georgia's upcoming ballot 'audit' a recount?*, AP (Nov. 12, 2020).

[242] *Risk-Limiting Audit Report, Georgia Presidential Contest, November 2020*, Georgia Sec. of State (Nov. 19, 2020) (Available at https://sos.ga.gov/admin/uploads/11.19_.20_Risk_Limiting_Audit_Report_Memo_1.pdf); Christina A. Cassidy, *EXPLAINER: Is Georgia's upcoming ballot 'audit' a recount?*, AP (Nov. 12, 2020).

[243] Kevin Bohn, *Trump campaign requests Georgia recount that's unlikely to change his loss in the state*, CNN (Nov. 22, 2020).

[244] Marshall Cohen et al, *Georgia's GOP governor and secretary of state certify Biden win, quashing Trump's longshot attempt to overturn results*, CNN (Nov. 20, 2020).

[245] David Morgan, *Georgia sets timeline for Trump-requested vote recount*, Reuters (Nov. 23, 2020).

[246] Richard Fausset & Nick Corasaniti, *Georgia Recertifies Election Results, Affirming Biden's Victory*, N. Y. Times (Dec. 7, 2020).

The final tally showed that President Trump lost the State of Georgia by 11,779 votes.[247] Georgia's slate of presidential electors then duly cast their votes on December 14, 2020 in accordance with the Electoral Count Act of 1887. During the post-election period, the Trump campaign and supporters of President Trump filed at least seven lawsuits in Georgia courts seeking to overturn the result in Georgia or otherwise challenge the conduct of the election, all of which were dismissed either by the court or voluntarily by the plaintiff.[248]

Against that background, on the afternoon of January 2, 2021, President Trump convened the call with Secretary Raffensperger. On the call he repeatedly urged the Secretary to accept or investigate claims of voting irregularities. The President insisted, "I think it's pretty clear that we won. We won very substantially in Georgia." The Secretary responded, "We don't agree that you have won," and explained that "the challenge that you have is the data you have is wrong." With respect to a claim made by President Trump that 5,000 votes were cast in Georgia by people recorded as having died, the Secretary explained that the state had investigated the matter and identified only two such votes. The President asserted that certain ballots were scanned three times. The Secretary responded, "We did an audit of that, and we proved conclusively that they were not scanned three times." The President and one of his attorneys also asserted that 4,500 voters had cast Georgia ballots after moving out of the state. The Secretary and a Georgia official explained in response that the state had been "going through each of those as well," and that "[e]very one we've been through are people that lived in Georgia, moved to a different state, but then moved back to Georgia legitimately."[249]

President Trump refused to accept Secretary Raffenberger's conclusion that he had not won the election. He told the Secretary that "the ballots are corrupt," that this was "totally illegal" and in fact "more illegal for you than it is for them" because "you're not reporting it." "That's a criminal, that's a criminal offense," he said, and "a big risk to you." He said that the state was "shredding ballots" and "removing machinery," and said, "I'm notifying you that you're letting it happen." And he told the Secretary, "So look. All I want to do is this. I just want to find 11,780 votes, which is one more than we have because we won the state."[250]

President Trump cared only that a state official certify that he won Georgia. He asked the Secretary to belatedly "find" new votes for him—just enough for him to win the state. He did not care about the actual results. He was indifferent to the truth or falsity of the unsupported claims of voting impropriety that he asserted. And to back up his demands, he threatened the Secretary, alluding to the possibility that his government would pursue criminal charges against him if he failed to "find" those votes.

This exchange comes on the heels of a call in late December in which President Trump was reported to have pressured a top Georgia election official, saying the investigator would be a

---

[247] Christina A. Cassidy, *EXPLAINER: Is Georgia's upcoming ballot 'audit' a recount?,* AP (Nov. 12, 2020).

[248] Pete Williams & Nicole Via y Rada, *Trump's election fight includes over 50 lawsuits. It's not going well.,* NBC (Nov. 23, 2020).

[249] Amy Gardner & Paulina Firozi, Here's the full transcript and audio of the call between Trump and Raffensperger, Wash. Post (Jan. 5, 2021).

[250] *Id.*

"'national hero' for finding evidence of fraud" and again claimed there were problems with the signature-matching system used by the state[251] This call was made as the state of Georgia conducted an audit of ballots in Cobb County. President Trump's exchanges with state officials also occurred in the context of reported White House pressure on the U.S. for the Northern District of Georgia Byung J. Pak, who abruptly resigned on January 5, 2020.[252] Pak was reported to have been forced to resign because he was not investigating the President's claims of widespread voter fraud in Georgia strongly enough.[253]

In sum, the President pressured the Secretary to conclude that he had won Georgia without regard to whether that was factually so. This conversation echoes other reported instances in which the President pressured officials and legislators in Georgia and other states,[254] and in the federal government, to alter the election outcome in his favor. Most recently, he urged the Vice-President of the United States to usurp an authority not granted to him by the Constitution to reject the votes of a state's duly appointed electors, and to cause President Trump to be wrongfully appointed as President; and when Mr. Pence refused to do so, he incited the armed mob of his followers to go to the Capitol to disrupt the proceedings.

President Trump's incitement of mob violence against the Capitol is clearly part of a broader pattern of encouraging lawless behavior and official action where it serves to aggrandize his own power. Especially in light of the accelerating pace of these events as the end of President Trump's term comes to a close, the risk that that pattern will continue and repeat itself even in the final days of his administration is great.

B. The Need to Establish Precedent That Such Conduct by a President Is Unconstitutional and Contrary to Our Democratic Values

The House must impeach President Trump to make clear for all future officeholders that our Constitution rejects President Trump's behavior. Since President Washington willingly relinquished his office at the end of his second term in 1797, this country has seen an unbroken chain of peaceful transitions. Some have argued that given the little remaining time left in President Trump's term, there is no need to impeach him now. This ignores the precedent this country would set if we refuse to impeach and the remedy of disqualification that the Senate may impose. Even wrongly assuming that President Trump poses no ongoing threat, impeachment sends the strongest

---

[251] Richard Fausset & Katie Benner, *Georgia Officials Reveal Third Trump Call Seeking to Influence Election Results,* N. Y. Times (Jan. 9, 2021).

[252] Kelly Mena, *Wall Street Journal: White House pressured Georgia federal prosecutor to resign,* CNN (Jan. 9, 2021).

[253] Aruna Viswanatha et al., *White House Forced Georgia U.S. Attorney to Resign,* Wall Street Journal (Jan. 9, 2021).

[254] See e.g., Carol D. Leonnig & Tom Hamburger, *Michigan attorney general ponders criminal probes of state and local officials who bend to Trump's will on overturning election results,* Wash. Post (Nov. 21, 2020); Alison Durkee, *Pennsylvania GOP lawmakers make clear they won't overturn the election as Trump wants,* Forbes (Dec. 3, 2020).

possible message that, as John Adams said, we are a "government of laws, and not of men."[255] Impeachment is a necessary measure to make sure that no President ever again attempts to incite his supporters to take unlawful action and overturn the will of the people. Indeed, the Constitution prohibits certain government officials who have "engaged in insurrection or rebellion" against the United States from holding "any office . . . under the United States."[256]

Impeachment is appropriate in the wake of this attack on the Capitol. The House has a solemn obligation to issue the appropriate charges and passing this article of impeachment preserves the ability of the Senate to take up the charges as it sees fit. This impeachment does not seek to undo an election. Rather, it seeks to vindicate the most recent election, protect it from a President who defies it, and protect future elections from presidents who may try to do the same. This impeachment is an essential statement about our Constitution and our democracy.

Courts across the country have rejected his false claims of fraud—and not just on procedural grounds. In Arizona, for example, the court found no fraud, no misconduct, no illegal votes, and confirmed that President-elect Biden won.[257] Likewise, in Wisconsin, the court heard President Trump's claims on the merits and rejected them.[258] Moreover, hand counts and hand audits in multiple states confirmed the accuracy of the vote. Other courts have ruled that the alleged claims of rigged voting machines pushed by President Trump and others are "implausible."[259] Those outcomes are part of the over 60 post-election cases decided adversely to President Trump and his allies. Yet he falsely and repeatedly screamed fraud, culminating in an appeal to his supporters to travel to Washington, D.C. on January 6th—where he told them to march to the Capitol and repeated his baseless claim that "we won in a landslide."

President Trump did not just falsely assert that he won the Presidency. He went much further. He pressured state officials to change the results and "find" more votes. He encouraged state officers not to exercise their ministerial duties. He told his supporters to assemble in Washington, D.C. on January 6th—the day of the Joint Session. He promised that it would be "wild." President Trump's goal was to disrupt the Joint Session of Congress that was meeting to formally count the electoral votes in an election that his opponent won.

President Trump also encouraged his Vice President to violate his own oath and claim unilateral authority to reject the votes of the Electoral College in an unconstitutional effort to declare President Trump the victor. Vice President Pence rightly rejected this view in his January 6, 2021 letter: "When disputes concerning a presidential election arise, under Federal law, it is the

---

[255] Papers of John Adams vol. 2 p. 314, Massachusetts Historical Society, available at http://www.masshist.org/publications/adams-papers/index.php/view/PJA02p314 .

[256] U.S. CONST. amend. XIV § 3.

[257] Bob Christie & Jacques Billeaud, *Arizona Supreme Court upholds election challenge dismissal*, AP (Jan. 5, 2021); Laura Gomez, Judge: No fraud, misconduct, illegal votes in Maricopa County's 2020 election, Arizona Mirror (Dec. 4, 2020).

[258] Adam Brewster, *Wisconsin Supreme Court rejects Trump campaign effort to toss ballots just before electors meet*, CBS News (Dec. 14, 2020).

[259] Jeremy Duda, *Attorney for Sec of State: 'Kraken' lawsuit alleges 'utterly implausible fraud'*, Arizona Mirror (Dec. 8, 2020).

people's representatives who review the evidence and resolve disputes through a democratic process."[260] As Vice President Pence concluded, "[v]esting the Vice President with unilateral authority to decide presidential contests would be entirely antithetical" to the Constitutional design.[261] Not only did President Trump encourage Vice President Pence to take that unconstitutional step, he pressured Vice President Pence and told his supporters that "if Mike Pence does the right thing, we win the election." And if he didn't do as Trump commanded, "Mike Pence . . . I'm going to be very disappointed in you."[262] Little wonder that when President Trump's supporters stormed the Capitol, some went looking for Vice President Pence.

[260] *Available at* Aaron Glantz, *Read Pence's full letter saying he can't claim 'unilateral authority' to reject electoral votes*, PBS (Jan. 6, 2021).

[261] *Id.*

[262] Julia Jacobo, *This is what Trump told supporters before many stormed Capitol Hill*, ABC News (Jan. 7, 2021)

<u>CONCLUSION</u>

In the words of Vice President Pence, the "Presidency belongs to the American people, and to them alone."[263] President Trump has falsely asserted he won the 2020 presidential election and repeatedly sought to overturn the results of the election. As his efforts failed again and again, President Trump continued a parallel course of conduct that foreseeably resulted in the imminent lawless actions of his supporters, who attacked the Capitol and the Congress. This course of conduct, viewed within the context of his past actions and other attempts to subvert the presidential election, demonstrate that President Trump remains a clear and present danger to the Constitution and our democracy. The House must reject this outrageous attempt to overturn the election and this incitement of violence by a sitting president against his own government. President Trump committed a high Crime and Misdemeanor against the Nation by inciting an insurrection at the Capitol in an attempt to overturn the results of the 2020 Presidential Election. The facts establish that he is unfit to remain in office a single day longer, and warrant the immediate impeachment of President Trump.

---

[263] *Available at* Aaron Glantz, *Read Pence's full letter saying he can't claim 'unilateral authority' to reject electoral votes*, PBS (Jan. 6, 2021).

APPENDIX

Public Reporting and Other Documents

Aaron Glantz, Read Pence's full letter saying he can't claim 'unilateral authority' to reject electoral votes, PBS (Jan. 6, 2021) (https://www.pbs.org/newshour/politics/read-pences-full-letter-saying-he-cant-claim-unilateral-authority-to-reject-electoral-votes)

Aaron Katersky & Celia Darrough, Armed protests being planned at all 50 state capitols, FBI bulletin says, ABC News (Jan. 11, 2021) (https://abcnews.go.com/US/armed-protests-planned-50-state-capitols-fbi-bulletin/story?id=75179771)

ACLU Again Calls for Impeachment of President Trump, ACLU Press Release (Jan. 10, 2021) (https://www.aclunc.org/news/aclu-again-calls-impeachment-president-trump)

A.C. Thompson & Ford Fischer, Members of Several Well-Known Hate Groups Identified at Capitol Riot, ProPublica (Jan. 9, 2021) (https://www.propublica.org/article/several-well-known-hate-groups-identified-at-capitol-riot?utm_source=sailthru&utm_medium=email&utm_campaign=majorinvestigations&utm_content=feature)

Acting Secretary Wolf Condemns Violence at The U.S. Capitol, Homeland Security (Jan. 7, 2021) (https://www.dhs.gov/news/2021/01/07/acting-secretary-wolf-condemns-violence-us-capitol)

Adam Brewster, Wisconsin Supreme Court rejects Trump campaign effort to toss ballots just before electors meet, CBS News (Dec. 14, 2020) (https://www.cbsnews.com/news/wisconsin-supreme-court-rejects-trump-election-campaign-effort-toss-ballots-before-electors-meet/)

Adam Johnson Statement of Facts (https://www.justice.gov/usao-dc/press-release/file/1351951/download)

Adam Rawnsley & Justin Rohrlich'Ready to Die': Two Months of MAGA Mob Warning Signs, The Daily Beast (Jan. 8, 2021) (https://www.thedailybeast.com/there-were-two-months-of-warning-signs-before-the-maga-mob-capitol-riot?ref=scroll)

Alan Feuer, Police Reassess Security for Inauguration and Demonstrations After Capitol Attack, N.Y. Times (Jan. 10, 2021) (https://www.nytimes.com/2021/01/10/us/inauguration-security-police.html?action=click&module=Spotlight&pgtype=Homepage)

Alexander Bolton, GOP Senator: Trump 'Committeed Impeachable Offenses', The Hill (Jan. 9, 2021) (https://thehill.com/homenews/senate/533498-gop-sen-toomey-trump-committed-impeachable-offenses)

Alexander Mallin and Luke Barr, Man Who Allegedly Broke Into Pelosi's Office Charged with 3 Federal Counts, ABC News (Jan. 9, 2021) (https://abcnews.go.com/Politics/man-broke-pelosis-office-charged-federal-counts/story?id=75137325)

Alexander Smith & Saphora Smith, U.S. foes like China and Iran see opportunity in the chaos of Trump-stoked riot at Capitol, NBC News, (Jan. 8, 2021) (https://www.nbcnews.com/news/world/u-s-foes-china-iran-see-opportunity-chaos-trump-stoked-n1253318)

Alison Durkee, Pennsylvania GOP lawmakers make clear they won't overturn the election as Trump wants, Forbes (Dec. 3, 2020) (https://www.forbes.com/sites/alisondurkee/2020/12/03/pennsylvania-gop-lawmakers-make-clear-they-wont-overturn-the-election-as-trump-wants/?sh=50f287102b39)

Allan Smith, D.C. Police make several arrests ahead of major pro-Trump election protest, NBC News (Jan. 5, 2021) (https://www.nbcnews.com/politics/donald-trump/dc-police-make-several-arrests-ahead-major-pro-trump-election-n1252938)

Allison Klein and Rebecca Tan, Capitol Police officer who was on duty during the riot has died by suicide, his family says, Wash. Post (Jan. 11, 2021) (https://www.washingtonpost.com/local/public-safety/liebengood-capitol-police-death/2021/01/10/3a495b84-5357-11eb-a08b-f1381ef3d207_story.html)

Amanda Macias, Mattis blames Trump for violence at Capitol, says his actions 'poison our respect for fellow citizens', CNBC (Jan. 6, 2021) (https://www.cnbc.com/2021/01/06/mattis-blames-trump-for-violence-at-capitol-says-his-actions-poison-our-respect-for-fellow-citizens.html)

Amanda Seitz, Mob at U.S. Capitol encouraged by online conspiracy theories, AP (Jan. 7, 2021) (https://apnews.com/article/donald-trump-conspiracy-theories-michael-pence-media-social-media-daba3f5dd16a431abc627a5cfc922b87)

Amy Brittain, et al., The Capitol mob: A raging collection of grievances and disillusionment, Wash. Post (Jan. 10, 2021) (https://www.washingtonpost.com/investigations/2021/01/10/capitol-rioters-identified-arrested/)

Amy Gardner, 'Find the fraud': Trump pressured a Georgia elections investigator in a separate call legal experts say could amount to obstruction, Wash. Post (Jan. 9, 2021) (https://www.washingtonpost.com/politics/trump-call-georgia-investigator/2021/01/09/7a55c7fa-51cf-11eb-83e3-322644d82356_story.html)

Amy Gardner and Keith Newell, 'Someone's going to get killed': GOP election official in Georgia blames President Trump for fostering violent threats, Wash. Post (Dec. 1, 2020) (https://www.washingtonpost.com/politics/georgia-official-trump-election/2020/12/01/f1d5c962-3427-11eb-b59c-adb7153d10c2_story.html)

Amy Gardner & Paulina Firozi, Here's the full transcript and audio of the call between Trump and Raffensperger, Wash. Post (Jan. 5, 2021) (https://www.washingtonpost.com/politics/trump-raffensperger-call-transcript-georgia-vote/2021/01/03/2768e0cc-4ddd-11eb-83e3-322644d82356_story.html)

Amy Gardner, 'I just want to find 11,780 votes': In extraordinary hour-long call, Trump pressures Georgia secretary of state to recalculate the vote in his favor, Wash. Post (Jan. 3, 2021) (https://www.washingtonpost.com/politics/trump-raffensperger-call-georgia-vote/2021/01/03/d45acb92-4dc4-11eb-bda4-615aaefd0555_story.html)

Andrew Beaujon, MAGA Geniuses Plot Takeover of US Capitol, Washingtonian (Jan. 5, 2021) (https://www.washingtonian.com/2021/01/05/maga-geniuses-plot-takeover-of-us-capitol/)

Andrew Prokop, Republican senator: White House aides say Trump was "delighted" as Capitol was stormed, Vox (Jan. 8, 2021) (https://www.vox.com/2021/1/8/22220840/sasse-trump-capitol-storming-impeachment)

Annie Palmer, Facebook will block Trump from posting at least for the remainder of his term, CNBC (Jan. 7, 2021) (https://www.cnbc.com/2021/01/07/facebook-will-block-trump-from-posting-for-the-remainder-of-his-term.html)

Aruna Viswanatha, Sadie Gurman & Cameron McWhirter, White House Forced Georgia U.S. Attorney to Resign, Wall Street Journal (Jan. 9, 2021) (https://www.wsj.com/articles/white-house-forced-georgia-u-s-attorney-to-resign-11610225840)

Ashley Parker et al., Six hours of paralysis: Inside Trump's failure to act after a mob stormed the Capitol, Wash. Post (Jan. 11, 2021) (https://www.washingtonpost.com/politics/trump-mob-failure/2021/01/11/36a46e2e-542e-11eb-a817-e5e7f8a406d6_story.html)

Associated Press, Judge bans Proud Boys leader from Washington, D.C., after arrest, NBC News (Jan. 5, 2021) (https://www.nbcnews.com/news/us-news/judge-bans-proud-boys-leader-washington-d-c-after-arrest-n1252906)

Associated Press, Trump doesn't ask backers to disperse after storming Capitol, PBS (Jan. 6, 2021) (https://www.pbs.org/newshour/politics/gop-lawmakers-ask-trump-to-deescalate-violence)

Azi Paybarah and Brent Lewis, Stunning Images as a Mob Storms the U.S. Capitol, N. Y. Times (Jan. 6, 2021) (https://www.nytimes.com/2021/01/06/us/politics/trump-riot-dc-capitol-photos.html)

Barry, McIntire, Rosenberg, 'Our President Wants Us Here': The Mob That Stormed the Capitol, N. Y. Times (Jan. 9, 2021) (https://www.nytimes.com/2021/01/09/us/capitol-rioters.html)

Ben Collins & Brandy Zadrozny, Extremists made little secret of ambitions to 'occupy' Capitol in weeks before attack, NBC News (Jan. 8, 2021) (https://www.nbcnews.com/tech/internet/extremists-made-little-secret-ambitions-occupy-capital-weeks-attack-n1253499)

Bernard Bailyn, The Ideological Origins of the American Revolution 282 (1967)

Betsy Devos Letter of Resignation (Jan. 7, 2021) (https://context-cdn.washingtonpost.com/notes/prod/default/documents/409afad4-abcd-4606-833a-682807a9a219/note/92c50db0-c1a9-4179-a478-c2891a13bf0e.#page=1)

Bob Christie & Jacques Billeaud, Arizona Supreme Court upholds election challenge dismissal, AP (Jan. 5, 2021) (https://apnews.com/article/election-2020-joe-biden-donald-trump-arizona-phoenix-e929a14f4dca0de3d9929fb4cef4a6fb)

Brandenburg v. Ohio, 395 U.S. 444 (1969) (https://supreme.justia.com/cases/federal/us/395/444/)

Brandy Zadronzyny & Ben Collins, Violent threats ripple through far-right internet forums ahead of protest, NBC (Jan. 5, 2020) (https://www.nbcnews.com/tech/internet/violent-threats-ripple-through-far-right-internet-forums-ahead-protest-n1252923)

Brian Fung, Capitol riots raise urgent concerns about Congress's information security, CNN (Jan. 8, 2021) (https://www.cnn.com/2021/01/07/tech/capitol-riots-cybersecurity/index.html)

Brian Shelter and Oliver Darcy, Even worse than it looked on live TV, CNN (Jan. 9, 2021) (https://view.newsletters.cnn.com/messages/1610170820900f85a0cb63e85/raw)

Carol D. Leonnig & Tom Hamburger, Michigan attorney general ponders criminal probes of state and local officials who bend to Trump's will on overturning election results, Wash. Post (Nov. 21, 2020) (https://www.washingtonpost.com/politics/michigan-attorney-general-canvassing-board-lawmakers/2020/11/20/87d19ce6-2b65-11eb-8fa2-06e7cbb145c0_story.html)

Carol D. Loennig et al, Outgoing Capitol Police chief: House, Senate security officials hamstrung efforts to call in National Guard, Wash. Post (Jan. 10, 2021) (https://www.washingtonpost.com/politics/sund-riot-national-guard/2021/01/10/fc2ce7d4-5384-11eb-a817-e5e7f8a406d6_story.html)

Carol Robinson, Lonnie Coffman, Alabama man arrested at DC riot, had homemade napalm in Mason jars, feds say, AL (Jan. 8, 2021) (https://www.al.com/news/birmingham/2021/01/lonnie-coffman-alabama-man-arrested-at-dc-riot-had-homemade-napalm-in-mason-jars-feds-say.html)

Cass Sunstein, Does the 25th Amendment Apply to Trump? Quite Possibly, Bloomberg (Jan. 7, 2021) (https://www.denverpost.com/2021/01/07/25th-amendment-donald-trump-coup-capitol-riot-protest/)

Caroline Linton, Capitol Police officer who responded to attack has died, CBS News (Jan. 11, 2021) (https://www.cbsnews.com/news/howard-liebengood-dies-capitol-police-officer-riots/)

Chelsea Stahl, Jan. 7 highlights and analysis of unrest in Washington, D.C., NBC (Jan. 8, 2021) (https://www.nbcnews.com/politics/congress/blog/2021-01-06-congress-electoral-vote-count-n1253179)

Chris Marquette et al., Pro-Trump protesters storm Capitol during Electoral College certification, causing lockdown, Roll Call (Jan. 6, 2021) (https://www.rollcall.com/2021/01/06/pro-trump-protestors-storm-capitol-during-electoral-college-certification-causing-capitol-lockdown/)

Chris Marquette, Katherine Tully-McManus, & Chris Cioffi, Pro-Trump protesters storm Capitol during Electoral College certification, causing lockdown, Roll Call (Jan. 6, 2021)

(https://www.rollcall.com/2021/01/06/pro-trump-protestors-storm-capitol-during-electoral-college-certification-causing-capitol-lockdown/)

Chris Sommerfeldt, Pro-Trump rioters smeared poop in U.S. Capitol hallways during belligerent attack, NY Daily News (Jan. 7, 2021) (https://www.nydailynews.com/news/politics/ny-trump-capitol-riot-poopers-20210107-prlsqytyabgdhnexushotl4nam-story.html)

Christina A. Cassidy, EXPLAINER: Is Georgia's upcoming ballot 'audit' a recount?, AP (Nov. 12, 2020) (https://apnews.com/article/ap-explains-georgia-audit-or-recount-9adf1d0ed50f8788572b4f7e0f04027e)

Christine Mui, Ex-Trump Chief of Staff John Kelly supports 25th Amendment to remove president, Boston Globe (Jan. 7, 2021) (https://www.bostonglobe.com/2021/01/07/metro/ex-trump-chief-staff-john-kelly-supports-25th-amendment-remove-president/)

Christopher Alberts Criminal Complaint (Jan. 7, 2021) (https://www.justice.gov/opa/press-release/file/1351681/download)

Cindy Fitchet, et al. Criminal Complaint (Jan. 7, 2021) (https://www.justice.gov/opa/press-release/file/1351716/download)

Cindy Fitchet, et al. Statement of Facts (Jan. 7, 2021) (https://www.justice.gov/opa/press-release/file/1351721/download)

Craig Timberg and Drew Harwell, Pro-Trump Forums Erupt with Violent Threats Ahead of Wednesday's Rally Against the 2020 Election, Wash. Post (Jan. 5, 2021) (https://www.washingtonpost.com/technology/2021/01/05/parler-telegram-violence-dc-protests/)

Dan Barry & Sheera Frenkel, 'Be There. Will Be Wild!': Trump All but Circled the Date, N. Y. Times (Jan. 6, 2021) (https://www.nytimes.com/2021/01/06/us/politics/capitol-mob-trump-supporters.html)

Dan Barry, Mike McIntire & Matthew Rosenberg, 'Our President Wants Us Here': The Mob That Stormed the Capitol, N. Y. Times (Jan. 9, 2021) (https://www.nytimes.com/2021/01/09/us/capitol-rioters.html)

Dan Packel, Thousands of Attorneys Join Calls for Trump's Immediate Removal, Law.com (Jan. 8, 2021) (https://www.law.com/nationallawjournal/2021/01/08/thousands-of-attorneys-join-calls-for-trumps-immediate-removal/)

David Choi, Trump lowers the White House flag after pressure from both Republicans and Democrats, Business Insider (Jan. 11, 2021) (https://www.businessinsider.in/politics/world/news/trump-lowers-the-white-house-flag-after-pressure-from-both-republicans-and-democrats/articleshow/80204385.cms.)

David Landau and Rosalind Dixon, The 25th Amendment Can Remove Trump, but We Shouldn't Stop There, N, Y. Times (Jan. 7, 2021) (https://www.nytimes.com/2021/01/07/opinion/trump-25th-amendment-impeachment.html)

David Morgan, Georgia sets timeline for Trump-requested vote recount, Reuters (Nov. 23, 2020). (https://www.reuters.com/article/us-usa-election-georgia-recount/georgia-sets-timeline-for-trump-requested-vote-recount-idUSKBN2832XC)

David Priess & Jack Goldsmith, Can Trump Be Stopped?, Lawfare (Jan. 7, 2021) (https://www.lawfareblog.com/can-trump-be-stopped)

David Smith et al., Donald Trump refuses to condemn white supremacists at presidential debate, The Guardian (Sep. 29, 2020) (https://www.theguardian.com/us-news/2020/sep/29/trump-proud-boys-debate-president-refuses-condemn-white-supremacists)

Devlin Barrett, Spencer S. Hsu & Matt Zapotosky, FBI focuses on whether some Capitol rioters intended to harm lawmakers or take hostages, Wash. Post (Jan.8, 2021) (https://www.washingtonpost.com/national-security/capitol-riot-fbi-hostages/2021/01/08/df99ae5a-5202-11eb-83e3-322644d82356_story.html)

Domenico Montanaro, Timeline: How One Of The Darkest Days In American History Unfolded, NPR (Jan. 7, 2021) (https://www.npr.org/2021/01/07/954384999/timeline-how-one-of-the-darkest-days-in-american-history-unfolded)

Ed Pilkington, Incitement: a timeline of Trump's inflammatory rhetoric before the Capitol riot, The Guardian (Jan. 7, 2021) (https://www.theguardian.com/us-news/2021/jan/07/trump-incitement-inflammatory-rhetoric-capitol-riot)

Elaine Godfrey, It was Supposed to be so Much Worse, The Atlantic (Jan. 9, 2021) (https://www.theatlantic.com/politics/archive/2021/01/trump-rioters-wanted-more-violence-worse/617614/)

Eliott C. McLaughlin, Before Wednesday, Insurgents Waving Confederate Flags Hadn't Been Within 6 Miles of the US Capitol, CNN (Jan. 7, 2021) (https://www.cnn.com/2021/01/07/us/capitol-confederate-flag-fort-stevens/index.html)

Eric Munchel Complaint (https://www.justice.gov/usao-dc/press-release/file/1352226/download)

Erin Schumaker, Trump officials who have resigned in the wake of attack on Capitol, ABC News (Jan. 9, 2021) (https://abcnews.go.com/Politics/trump-officials-resigned-wake-attack-capitol/story?id=75108384)

Evan Hill et al., 'They Got a Officer!': How a Mob Dragged and Beat Police at the Capitol, N. Y. Times (Jan. 11, 2021) (https://www.nytimes.com/2021/01/11/us/capitol-mob-violence-police.html)

Extremists and Mainstream Trump Supporters Plan to Protest Congressional Certification of Biden's Victory, ADL (Jan. 4, 2021) (https://www.adl.org/blog/extremists-and-mainstream-trump-supporters-plan-to-protest-congressional-certification-of)

Fandos, Schaff, and Cochrane, 'Senate Being Locked Down': Inside a Harrowing Day at the Capitol, N. Y. Times (Jan. 7, 2021) (https://www.nytimes.com/2021/01/07/us/politics/capitol-lockdown.html)

Foreign Ministry Spokesperson Hua Chunying's Regular Press Conference on January 7, 2021, Ministry of Foreign Affairs of the People's Republic of China (Jan. 7, 2021) (http://www.china-embassy.org/eng/fyrth/t1845062.htm)

Frank O. Bowman, III, The Constitutional Case for Impeaching Donald Trump (Again), Just Security (Jan. 9, 2021) (https://www.justsecurity.org/74127/the-constitutional-case-for-impeaching-donald-trump-again/)

George Petras, et al., Timeline: How a Trump mob stormed the US Capitol, forcing Washington into lockdown, USA TODAY (Jan. 8, 2021) (https://www.usatoday.com/in-depth/news/2021/01/06/dc-protests-capitol-riot-trump-supporters-electoral-college-stolen-election/6568305002)

Glenn Thrush and Maggie Haberman, Trump Gives White Supremacists an Unequivocal Boost, N. Y. Times (Aug. 15, 2017) (https://www.nytimes.com/2017/08/15/us/politics/trump-charlottesville-white-nationalists.html)

Helene Cooper et al., As the D.C. police clear the Capitol grounds, the mayor extends a public emergency, N. Y. Times (Jan. 6, 2021) (https://www.nytimes.com/2021/01/06/us/politics/national-guard-capitol-army.html)

Ilya Somin, A Qualified Defense of Impeaching Trump Again, Reason (Jan. 6, 2021) (https://reason.com/volokh/2021/01/06/a-qualified-defense-of-impeaching-trump)

Ilya Somin, The First Amendment Doesn't Protect Trump Against Impeachment for his Role in Inciting the Assault on the Capitol, The Volokh Conspiracy (January 8, 2021) (https://reason.com/volokh/2021/01/08/the-first-amendment-doesnt-protect-trump-against-impeachment-for-his-role-in-inciting-the-assault-on-the-capitol/)

Jack Brewster & Andrew Solender, Clyburn's Ipad, Laptop From Pelosi's Office: Items Stolen, Destroyed In Capitol Attack, Forbes (Jan. 7, 2021) (https://www.forbes.com/sites/jackbrewster/2021/01/08/clyburns-ipad-laptop-from-pelosis-office-items-stolen-destroyed-in-capitol-attack/?sh=44112d1c5963)

James Brooks, Alaska Sen. Lisa Murkowski calls on President Trump to resign, questions her future as a Republican, Anchorage Daily News (Jan. 9, 2021) (https://www.adn.com/politics/2021/01/08/alaska-sen-lisa-murkowski-calls-on-president-trump-to-resign-questions-her-future-as-a-republican/)

Jason Hanna, Kaylee Hartung, Devon M. Sayers and Steve Almasy, Virginia governor to white nationalists: 'Go home … shame on you', CNN (Aug. 13, 2017) (https://www.cnn.com/2017/08/12/us/charlottesville-white-nationalists-rally/index.html)

Jennifer Berry & Thomas Novelly, Nancy Mace's first 100 hours in Congress: threats, violence and challenging Trump, The Post and Courier (Jan. 7, 2021) (https://www.postandcourier.com/politics/nancy-maces-first-100-hours-in-congress-threats-violence-and-challenging-trump/article_c7f17e0a-512a-11eb-bb95-7f8aa88739fb.html)

Jennifer Schuessler, Hundreds of Historians Join Call for Trump's Impeachment, N. Y. Times (Jan. 11, 2021) (https://www.nytimes.com/2021/01/11/arts/historians-impeachment.html)

Jeremy Duda, Attorney for Sec of State: 'Kraken' lawsuit alleges 'utterly implausible fraud', Arizona Mirror (Dec. 8, 2020) (https://www.azmirror.com/2020/12/08/attorney-for-sec-of-state-kraken-lawsuit-alleges-utterly-implausible-fraud/)

Jill Colvin, Hurt Feelings, Anger Linger After Pence, Trump Clash, ABC News (Jan. 8, 2021) (https://abcnews.go.com/Politics/wireStory/hurt-feelings-anger-linger-pence-trump-clash-75127167)

Jill Colvin & Zeke Miller, Pence defies Trump, affirms Biden's win, AP (Jan. 7, 2021) (https://apnews.com/article/mike-pence-electoral-vote-d27490021b4203087043df1939b82f8b)

John Podhoretz, Donald Trump Should Be Impeached and Removed from Office Tomorrow, Commentary Magazine (Jan. 6, 2021) (https://abcnews.go.com/Politics/wireStory/hurt-feelings-anger-linger-pence-trump-clash-75127167)

Jon Swaine, Dalton Bennett, Joyce Sohyun Lee & Meg Kelly, Video shows fatal shooting of Ashli Babbitt in the Capitol, WashPo (Jan. 8, 2021) (https://www.washingtonpost.com/investigations/2021/01/08/ashli-babbitt-shooting-video-capitol/)

Jonathan H. Adler, Yes, Congress May Impeach and Remove President Trump for Inciting Lawless Behavior at the Capitol, The Volokh Conspiracy (January 8, 2021) (https://reason.com/volokh/2021/01/08/yes-congress-may-impeach-and-remove-president-trump-for-inciting-lawless-behavior-at-the-capitol/)

John Hendrickson, Jamie Raskin Lost His Son. Then He Fled a Mob., The Atlantic (Jan. 8, 2021) (https://www.theatlantic.com/politics/archive/2021/01/jamie-raskin-capitol-attack/617609/)

Joshua Pruitt Criminal Complaint (https://www.justice.gov/opa/press-release/file/1351696/download)

Joshua Pruitt Statement of Facts (https://www.justice.gov/opa/press-release/file/1351701/download)

Julia Jacobo, A visual timeline on how the attack on Capitol Hill unfolded, ABC News (Jan. 10, 2021) (https://abcnews.go.com/US/visual-timeline-attack-capitol-hill-unfolded/story?id=75112066)

Julia Jacobo, This is what Trump told supporters before many stormed Capitol Hill, ABC News (Jan. 7, 2021) (https://abcnews.go.com/Politics/trump-told-supporters-stormed-capitol-hill/story?id=75110558)

Justine Coleman, Liz Cheney blames Trump for riots: 'He lit the flame', The Hill (Jan. 6, 2021) (https://thehill.com/homenews/house/533024-liz-cheney-blames-trump-for-riots-he-lit-the-flame)

Katie Shepherd, Video shows Capitol mob dragging police officer down stairs. One rioter beat the officer with a pole flying the U.S. flag, Wash. Post (Jan. 11, 2021) (https://www.washingtonpost.com/nation/2021/01/11/police-beating-capitol-mob/)

Karoun Demirjian et al., Inside the Capitol siege: How barricaded lawmakers and aides sounded urgent pleas for help as police lost control, Wash. Post (Jan. 10, 2021) (https://www.washingtonpost.com/politics/inside-capitol-siege/2021/01/09/e3ad3274-5283-11eb-bda4-615aaefd0555_story.html)

Keith E. Whittington, The conservative case for impeaching Trump now, Wash. Post (Jan. 7, 2021) (https://www.washingtonpost.com/outlook/2021/01/07/impeachment-trump-riot-conservative-case/)

Kel McClanahan, The MAGA Insurrection in the Capitol Created a Huge New National-Security Threat, Daily Beast (Jan. 8, 2021) (https://www.thedailybeast.com/the-maga-insurrection-in-the-capitol-created-a-huge-new-national-security-threat)

Kelly McLaughlin, The rioter who took photos at Nancy Pelosi's desk and recently said he's a white nationalist prepared for a violent death has been arrested, Business Insider (Jan. 8, 2021) (https://www.businessinsider.com/richard-barnett-self-proclaimed-white-nationalist-pictured-pelosi-desk-2021-1)

Kelly Mena, Wall Street Journal: White House pressured Georgia federal prosecutor to resign, CNN (Jan. 9, 2021) (https://www.cnn.com/2021/01/09/politics/white-house-trump-georgia-us-attorney-resigns/index.html)

Ken Dilanian et al., FBI, NYPD told Capitol Police about possibility of violence before riot, senior officials say, NBC News (Jan. 10, 2021) (https://www.nbcnews.com/news/crime-courts/fbi-nypd-told-capitol-police-about-possibility-violence-riot-senior-n1253646)

Kevin Bohn, Trump campaign requests Georgia recount that's unlikely to change his loss in the state, CNN (Nov. 22, 2020) (https://www.cnn.com/2020/11/21/politics/georgia-presidential-election-recount/index.html)

Kevin Liptak & Betsy Klein, Defiant Trump denounces violence but takes no responsibility for inciting deadly riot, CNN (Jan. 12, 2021). (https://www.cnn.com/2021/01/12/politics/donald-trump-riot-impeachment/index.html)

Kevin Liptak, Kaitlan Collins and Jeremy Diamond, Some Trump administration officials resign while others stay to prevent chaos, CNN (Jan. 7, 2021) (https://www.cnn.com/2021/01/07/politics/resignations-trump-white-house/index.html)

Kim Bellware, Police departments across the U.S. open probes into whether their own members took part in the Capitol riot, Wash. Post (Jan. 9, 2021) (https://www.washingtonpost.com/national-security/2021/01/09/investigating-police-rioters/)

Larry Brock Complaint (https://www.justice.gov/usao-dc/press-release/file/1352016/download)

Lauren Giella, Fact Check: Did Trump Call in the National Guard After Rioters Stormed the Capitol?, Newsweek (Jan. 8, 2021) (https://www.newsweek.com/fact-check-did-trump-call-national-guard-after-rioters-stormed-capitol-1560186)

Laura Gomez, Judge: No fraud, misconduct, illegal votes in Maricopa County's 2020 election, Arizona Mirror (Dec. 4, 2020) (https://www.azmirror.com/2020/12/04/judge-no-fraud-misconduct-illegal-votes-in-maricopa-countys-2020-election/)

Lauren Egan, Capitol reels from damage and destruction left by violent rioters, NBC (Jan. 7, 2021) (https://www.nbcnews.com/politics/congress/capitol-reels-damage-destruction-left-violent-rioters-n1253383)

Laurence H. Tribe & Joshua Matz, To End A Presidency: The Power of Impeachment 8565 (2018)

Laurence H. Tribe & Joshua Matz, Yes, Congress should impeach Trump before he leaves office, Wash. Post (Jan. 8, 2021) (https://www.washingtonpost.com/opinions/laurence-tribe-joshua-matz-impeach-trump-before-he-leaves-office/2021/01/08/70d7246c-5206-11eb-bda4-615aaefd0555_story.html)

Lonnie Coffman Criminal Complaint (https://www.justice.gov/opa/press-release/file/1351666/download)

Loss of USCP Officer Brian D. Sicknick, United States Capitol Police Press Release (Jan. 7, 2021) (https://www.uscp.gov/media-center/press-releases/loss-uscp-colleague-brian-d-sicknick)

Maggie Haberman, Trump Told Crowd 'You Will Never Take Back Our Country With Weakness,' N. Y. Times (Jan. 6, 2021) (https://www.nytimes.com/2021/01/06/us/politics/trump-speech-capitol.html)

Malachi Barrett, Michigan representatives denounce attack on U.S. Capitol by pro-Trump mob, MLive (Jan. 6, 2021) (https://www.mlive.com/politics/2021/01/michigan-representatives-denounce-attack-on-us-capitol-by-pro-trump-mob.html)

Marc Fisher et al., The four-hour insurrection, Wash. Post (Jan. 7, 2021) (https://www.washingtonpost.com/graphics/2021/politics/trump-insurrection-capitol/)

Mark Leffingwell Criminal Complaint (https://www.justice.gov/opa/press-release/file/1351671/download)

Mark Leffingwell Statement of Facts (https://www.justice.gov/opa/press-release/file/1351676/download)

Mark Mazzetti et al., Inside a Deadly Siege: How a String of Failures Led to a Dark Day at the Capitol, N.Y. Times (Jan. 10, 2021) (https://www.nytimes.com/2021/01/10/us/politics/capitol-siege-security.html?smid=tw-share)

Marshall Cohen et al, Georgia's GOP governor and secretary of state certify Biden win, quashing Trump's longshot attempt to overturn results, CNN (Nov. 20, 2020)

(https://www.cnn.com/2020/11/20/politics/georgia-certify-secretary-of-state-raffensperger/index.html)

Matt Fuller, House Democrats Briefed On 3 Terrifying Plots To Overthrow Government, Huff Post (Jan. 12, 2021) (https://www.huffpost.com/entry/democrats-briefed-plot-overthrow-government_n_5ffd29a4c5b691806c4bf199)

Matt Zapotosky & Tom Hamburger, Federal prosecutors assigned to monitor election malfeasance tell Barr they see no evidence of substantial irregularities, Wash. Post (Nov. 13, 2020) (https://www.washingtonpost.com/national-security/william-barr-election-memo/2020/11/13/6ed06d20-25e4-11eb-a688-5298ad5d580a_story.html)

Matthew Brown, Trump campaign lawyer stirs outrage by saying ex-cyber chief should be 'taken out at dawn and shot', USA Today (Dec. 1, 2020) (https://www.usatoday.com/story/news/politics/elections/2020/12/01/trump-campaign-lawyer-digenova-says-ex-cyber-chief-should-shot/6475099002/)

Matthew Council Criminal Complaint (https://www.justice.gov/opa/press-release/file/1351706/download)

Matthew Council Statement of Facts (https://www.justice.gov/opa/press-release/file/1351711/download)

Matthew S. Schwartz, As Inauguration Nears, Concern Of More Violence Grows, NPR (Jan. 9, 2021) (https://www.npr.org/sections/congress-electoral-college-tally-live-updates/2021/01/09/955289141/as-inauguration-nears-concern-grows-of-more-violence-to-come)

Mayor Bowser Continues Preparation for Upcoming First Amendment Demonstrations, Executive Office of the Mayor (Jan. 3, 2021) (https://mayor.dc.gov/release/mayor-bowser-continues-preparation-upcoming-first-amendment-demonstrations)

Melissa De Witte and Sharon Driscoll, Stanford Scholars React to Capitol Hill Takeover, Stanford News (Jan. 6, 2021) (https://news.stanford.edu/2021/01/06/stanford-scholars-react-capitol-hill-takeover/)

Michael Balsamo, Disputing Trump, Barr says no widespread election fraud., AP (Dec. 1, 2020) (https://apnews.com/article/barr-no-widespread-election-fraud-b1f1488796c9a98c4b1a9061a6c7f49d)

Michael Biesecker, Records show fervent Trump fans fueled US Capitol takeover, AP (Jan. 11, 2021) (https://apnews.com/article/us-capitol-trump-supporters-1806ea8dc15a2c04f2a68acd6b55cace)

Michael Levenson, Today's Rampage at the Capitol, as It Happened, N. Y. Times (Jan. 6, 2021) (https://www.nytimes.com/live/2021/01/06/us/washington-dc-protests)

Michael Phillips and Jennifer Levitz, One Trump Fan's Descent Into the U.S. Capitol Mob, Wall Street Journal (Jan. 10, 2021) (https://www.wsj.com/articles/one-trump-fans-descent-into-the-u-s-capitol-mob-11610311660)

Michael Stokes Paulsen, The Constitutional and Moral Imperative of Immediate Impeachment, The Bulwark (Jan. 8, 2021) (https://thebulwark.com/the-constitutional-and-moral-imperative-of-immediate-impeachment/)

Mike Isaac and Kate Conger, Facebook Bars Trump Through End of His Term, N. Y. Times (Jan. 8, 2021) (https://www.nytimes.com/2021/01/07/technology/facebook-trump-ban.html)

Mike Snider, President Trump deletes tweets after Twitter, Facebook and Instagram lock down accounts for 'violations', USA Today (Jan. 6, 2021) (https://www.usatoday.com/story/tech/2021/01/06/twitter-locks-president-trumps-account-after-his-tweets-riots/6574242002/)

Natalie Colarossi, Bar Association Urged to Disqulify Giuliani Over 'Trial by Combat' Speech Before D.C. Riot, Newsweek (Jan. 9, 2021) (https://www.newsweek.com/bar-association-urged-disqualify-giuliani-over-trial-combat-speech-before-dc-riot-1560263)

Natasha Bertrand, Justice Department warns of national security fallout from Capitol Hill insurrection, POLITICO (Jan. 7, 2021) (https://www.politico.com/news/2021/01/07/capitol-hill-riots-doj-456178)

NBC News, Highlights and Analysis: Trump Commits to 'Orderly Transition' After Mob Storms Capitol, NBC News (Jan. 7, 2021) (https://www.nbcnews.com/politics/congress/blog/electoral-college-certification-updates-n1252864)

Noah Feldman, I Testified at Trump's Last Impeachment. Impeach Him Again, Bloomberg (Jan. 7, 2021) (https://www.bloomberg.com/opinion/articles/2021-01-07/u-s-capitol-riot-incited-by-trump-is-his-latest-impeachable-offense)

Norman Eisen, The riot happened because the Senate acquitted Trump, Wash Post (Jan. 8, 2021) (https://www.washingtonpost.com/outlook/impeachment-senate-trump-acquitted/2021/01/08/157fb03e-515c-11eb-bda4-615aaefd0555_story.html)

"Objections" at the Joint Session of Congress: Countering the Lies, Voter Protection Program (Jan. 6, 2021) (https://voterprotectionprogram.org/wp-content/uploads/2021/01/000A-Myths-and-Facts-of-the-2020-Presidential-Election-20210105.docx80-FINAL1.pdf)

Officer Alexandria Sims Affidavit (Jan. 7, 2021) (https://assets.documentcloud.org/documents/20446053/blair_affidavit.pdf)

Officer Dallan Haynes Statement of Facts (Jan. 7, 2021) (https://www.justice.gov/opa/press-release/file/1351686/download)

Officer Christopher Frank Affidavit (Jan. 6, 2021) (https://beta.documentcloud.org/documents/20446048-sinclair_affidavit)

Oma Seddiq, Sen. Lindsey Graham blames Trump for Capitol riots and says the president needs to 'understand that his actions were the problem', Business Insider (Jan. 7, 2021) (https://www.businessinsider.com/lindsey-graham-trump-should-know-that-his-actions-were-the-problem-2021-1)

Orion Rummler, Barr condemns Trump: "Orchestrating a mob to pressure Congress is inexcusable", Axios (Jan. 7, 2021) (https://www.axios.com/trump-barr-capitol-mob-73da61e7-370b-4cc8-873f-fa19a885a2cd.html)

Our Response to the Violence in Washington, Facebook (Jan. 6, 2021) (https://about.fb.com/news/2021/01/responding-to-the-violence-in-washington-dc/)

Paul Schwartzman, Assessing the damage at the U.S. Capitol: 'You can see the broken windows', Wash Post. (Jan. 7, 2021) (https://www.washingtonpost.com/local/capitol-cleanup-washington/2021/01/07/4497d4f4-50fe-11eb-83e3-322644d82356_story.html?utm_source=twitter&utm_medium=social&utm_campaign=wp_main)

Pete Williams & Nicole Via y Rada, Trump's election fight includes over 50 lawsuits. It's not going well, NBC News (Nov. 23, 2020) (https://www.nbcnews.com/politics/2020-election/trump-s-election-fight-includes-over-30-lawsuits-it-s-n1248289)

Peter Hermann & Julia Zauzmer, Beaten, sprayed with mace and hit with stun guns: police describe injuries to dozens of officers during assault on U.S. Capitol, Wash. Post (Jan. 11, 2021). (https://www.washingtonpost.com/local/public-safety/police-capitol-injuires-trump/2021/01/11/ca68e3e2-5438-11eb-a08b-f1381ef3d207_story.html)

Philip Rucker, Ashley Parker & Josh Dawsey, After inciting mob attack, Trump retreats in rage. Then, grudgingly, he admits his loss, Wash. Post (Jan. 7, 2021) (https://www.washingtonpost.com/politics/trump-rage-riot/2021/01/07/26894c54-5108-11eb-b96e-0e54447b23a1_story.html)

Priscilla Alvarez & Geneva Sands, Acting Secretary of Homeland Security Chad Wolf resigns; FEMA Administrator Pete Gaynor to take over, CNN (Jan. 11, 2021) (https://www.cnn.com/2021/01/11/politics/chad-wolf-homeland-security/index.html)

Quint Forgey, Barr: Trump committed 'betrayal of his office', Politico (Jan. 7, 2021) (https://www.politico.com/news/2021/01/07/barr-trump-committed-betrayal-of-his-office-455812)

Rebecca Shabad, Noose appears near Capitol; protesters seen carrying Confederate flags, NBC News (Jan. 6, 2021) (https://www.nbcnews.com/politics/congress/live-blog/electoral-college-certification-updates-n1252864/ncrd1253129#blogHeader)

Rebecca Traister, 'It Was No Accident' Congresswoman Pramila Jayapal on surviving the siege, The Cut (Jan. 8, 2021) (https://www.thecut.com/2021/01/pramila-jayapal-surviving-capitol-riots.html)

Richard Barnett Statement of Facts (https://www.justice.gov/opa/press-release/file/1351656/download?utm_medium=email&utm_source=govdelivery)

Richard Barnett Complaint (https://www.justice.gov/opa/press-release/file/1351651/download)

Richard Fausset, Georgia Republicans Contort Themselves to Avoid Trump's Fury, N. Y. Times (Dec. 2, 2020) (https://www.nytimes.com/2020/12/02/us/politics/georgia-republicans-election-trump.html)

Richard Fausset & Katie Benner, Georgia Officials Reveal Third Trump Call Seeking to Influence Election Results, N. Y. Times (Jan. 9, 2021) (https://www.nytimes.com/2021/01/09/us/georgia-presidential-election-results.html)

Richard Fausset & Nick Corasaniti, Georgia Recertifies Election Results, Affirming Biden's Victory, N. Y. Times (Dec. 7, 2020) (https://www.nytimes.com/2020/12/07/us/politics/georgia-recertify-election-results.html)

Rick Massimo, Hogan: Federal approval to send National Guard during Capitol attack delayed, WTOP News (Jan. 7, 2021) (https://wtop.com/maryland/2021/01/hogan-federal-approval-to-send-national-guard-during-capitol-attack-delayed/)

Risk-Limiting Audit Report, Georgia Presidential Contest, November 2020, Georgia Sec. of State (Nov. 19, 2020) (https://sos.ga.gov/admin/uploads/11.19_.20_Risk_Limiting_Audit_Report_Memo_1.pdf)

Romney Condemns Insurrection at U.S. Capitol, Senator Mitt Romney: Press Releases (Jan. 6, 2021) (https://www.romney.senate.gov/romney-condemns-insurrection-us-capitol)

Ronan Farrow, An Air Force Combat Veteran Breached the Senate, The New Yorker (Jan. 9, 2021) (https://www.newyorker.com/news/news-desk/an-air-force-combat-veteran-breached-the-senate)

Rose Minutaglio, Rep. Susan Wild on the 'Sheer Panic' She Felt in that Viral Photo, Elle (Jan. 7, 2021) (https://www.elle.com/culture/career-politics/a35151993/susan-wild-capitol-lockdown-interview/)

Rudy Giuliani Speech Transcript at Trump's Washington, D.C. Rally: Wants 'Trial by Combat, Rev (Jan. 6, 2021) (https://www.rev.com/blog/transcripts/rudy-giuliani-speech-transcript-at-trumps-washington-d-c-rally-wants-trial-by-combat)

Ryan Goodman et al., Incitement Timeline: Year of Trump's Actions Leading to the Attack on the Capitol, Just Security (Jan. 11, 2021) (https://www.justsecurity.org/74138/incitement-timeline-year-of-trumps-actions-leading-to-the-attack-on-the-capitol/)

Salvador Rodriguez, Trump tweets from POTUS handle account, says looking 'at the possibilities of building out our own platform', CNBC (Jan. 8, 2021) (https://www.cnbc.com/2021/01/08/trump-tweets-from-potus-handle-account-says-looking-at-the-possibilities-of-building-out-our-own-platform.html)

Sarah Bahr, Curators Scour Capitol for Damage to the Building or Its Art, N. Y. Times (Jan. 7, 2021) (https://www.nytimes.com/2021/01/07/arts/design/us-capitol-art-damage.html)

Scott Wartman, Boehner: 'The GOP must awaken.' Former Speaker of the House slams the Republican Party over 'nightmare.', Cincinnati Enquirer (Jan. 7, 2021) (https://www.cincinnati.com/story/news/politics/2021/01/07/john-boehner-former-house-speaker-says-republican-party-must-awaken/6583413002/)

Serfaty, Cole & Rogers, As riot raged at Capitol, Trump tried to call senators to overturn election, CNN (Jan. 8, 2021) (https://www.cnn.com/2021/01/08/politics/mike-lee-tommy-tuberville-trump-misdialed-capitol-riot/index.html)

Shelly Tan et al., How one of America's ugliest days unraveled inside and outside the Capitol, Wash. Post (Jan. 9, 2021). (https://www.washingtonpost.com/nation/interactive/2021/capitol-insurrection-visual-timeline/)

Sonam Sheth et al., House and Senate abruptly go into recess after Trump-supporting rioters storm the Capitol building, Business Insider (Jan. 6, 2021) (https://www.businessinsider.com/house-senate-go-into-recess-amid-trump-supporter-protests-2021-1)

Special Agent Carlos D. Fontanez Affidavit (Jan, 10, 2021) (https://www.justice.gov/usao-dc/press-release/file/1352221/download)

Special Agent David J. Dimarco Affidavit (Jan. 8, 2021) (https://www.justice.gov/usao-dc/press-release/file/1351946/download)

Special Agent James Soltes Affidavit (Jan. 8, 2021) (https://www.justice.gov/usao-dc/press-release/file/1351941/download.)

Special Agent Lawrence Anyaso Affidavit (Jan. 7, 2021) (https://www.justice.gov/opa/press-release/file/1351661/download)

Special Agent Milagro Garcia Affidavit (Jan. 9, 2021) (https://www.justice.gov/usao-dc/press-release/file/1352026/download)

Stanford Law's Michael McConnell on the 25th Amendment and Trump, Stanford Law School (Jan. 7, 2021) (https://law.stanford.edu/2021/01/07/stanford-laws-michael-mcconnell-on-the-25th-amendment-and-trump/)

Statement by Acting Secretary Miller on Full Activation of D.C. National Guard, U.S. Dept. of Defense (Jan. 6, 2021) (https://www.defense.gov/Newsroom/Releases/Release/Article/2464427/statement-by-acting-secretary-miller-on-full-activation-of-dc-national-guard/)

Statement of Rep. Cheney (https://www.nytimes.com/2021/01/06/us/politics/trump-speech-capitol.html.)

Statement of Sen. Sasse (https://www.npr.org/sections/congress-electoral-college-tally-live-updates/2021/01/08/954854250/gop-sen-sasse-rips-trump-for-stoking-mob-calls-hawleys-objection-really-dumbass)

Statement of Steven Sund, Chief of Police, Regarding the Events of January 6, 2021, United States Capitol Police (Jan. 7, 2021) (https://www.uscp.gov/media-center/press-releases/statement-steven-sund-chief-police)

Steve Inskeep, Ben Sasse Rips Trump For Stoking Mob, Calls Josh Hawley's Objection 'Really Dumbass', NPR (Jan. 8, 2021) (https://www.npr.org/sections/congress-electoral-college-tally-live-updates/2021/01/08/954854250/gop-sen-sasse-rips-trump-for-stoking-mob-calls-hawleys-objection-really-dumbass)

Steve Mistler, Susan Collins: Trump 'Does Bear Responsibility' For Insurrection, Maine Public (Jan. 6, 2021) (https://www.mainepublic.org/post/susan-collins-trump-does-bear-responsibility-insurrection)

Sunlen Serfaty, Devan Cole & Alex Rogers, As riot raged at Capitol, Trump tried to call senators to overturn election, CNN (Jan. 8, 2021) (https://www.cnn.com/2021/01/08/politics/mike-lee-tommy-tuberville-trump-misdialed-capitol-riot/index.html)

Tasneem Nashrulla, Members Of Congress Described What It Was Like When A Pro-Trump Mob Stormed The Capitol, Buzzfeed (Jan. 6, 2021) (https://www.buzzfeednews.com/article/tasneemnashrulla/congress-members-describe-pro-trump-riot-capitol)

Ted Barrett et al., US Capitol secured, 4 dead after rioters stormed the halls of Congress to block Biden's win, CNN (Jan. 7, 2021) (https://www.cnn.com/2021/01/06/politics/us-capitol-lockdown/index.html)

The Diplomat, What Are Asian Governments Saying About the Storming of the US Capitol?, The Diplomat (Jan. 8, 2021) (https://thediplomat.com/2021/01/what-are-asian-governments-saying-about-the-storming-of-the-us-capitol/)

The New York Times, Twitter locks Trump's account after he encouraged his supporters to 'remember this day.', N. Y. Times (Jan. 8, 2021) (https://www.nytimes.com/2021/01/06/us/politics/twitter-deletes-trump-tweet.html)

The White House, Memorandum of Telephone Conversation: Telephone Conversation with President Zelenskyy of Ukraine (July 25, 2019) (https://www.whitehouse.gov/wp-content/uploads/2019/09/Unclassified09.2019.pdf)

Tony Keith, Twitter 'locks' President Trump for 12 hours Wednesday evening, KKTV (Jan. 6, 2021) (https://www.kktv.com/2021/01/06/president-trump-via-a-video-message-tells-supporters-to-go-home/)

William Cummings, et al., By the numbers: President Donald Trump's failed efforts to overturn the election, USA Today (Jan. 6, 2021) (https://www.usatoday.com/in-depth/news/politics/elections/2021/01/06/trumps-failed-efforts-overturn-election-numbers/4130307001/)

Wisconsin State Journal Editorial Board, Mike Gallagher is right: 'Call it off, Mr. President', Wisconsin State Journal (Jan. 6, 2021) (https://madison.com/wsj/opinion/editorial/mike-gallagher-is-right-call-it-off-mr-president/article_8eb72914-63d5-5c5a-882c-2f486921eb6c.html)

Zack Budryk, Hoyer says rioters destroyed display commemorating John Lewis, The Hill (Jan. 7, 2021) (https://thehill.com/homenews/house/533142-hoyer-says-rioters-destroyed-display-commemorating-john-lewis)

Zolan Kanno-Youngs et al., As House Was Breached, a Fear 'We'd Have to Fight' to Get Out, N. Y. Times (Jan. 6, 2021) (https://www.nytimes.com/2021/01/06/us/politics/capitol-breach-trump-protests.html)

Tweets

Borzou Daragahi (@borzoi), Twitter (Nov. 5, 2020, 10:14 AM)
(https://twitter.com/borzou/status/1324369493901123584?s=20)

CBS News (@CBSNews), Twitter (Jan. 6, 2021 3:56 PM)
(https://twitter.com/CBSNews/status/1346923577245896705)

Chris Megerian (@ChrisMegerian), Twitter (Jan. 7, 2021, 11:32 AM)
(https://twitter.com/ChrisMegerian/status/1347219541487734785)

CNN Tonight (@CNNTonight), Twitter (Jan. 8, 2021, 11:37PM)
(https://twitter.com/CNNTonight/status/1347764478872608771)

DC Police Department (@DCPoliceDept), Twitter (Jan. 7, 2021, 1:52 PM)
(https://twitter.com/DCPoliceDept/status/1347254914993549312)

DC Police Department (@DCPoliceDept), Twitter (Jan. 8, 2021, 10:52 AM)
(https://twitter.com/DCPoliceDept/status/1347571797429018625)

Donald J. Trump (@realDonaldTrump), Twitter (Dec. 13, 2020, 5:15 PM)
(http://www.trumptwitterarchive.com/archive)

Donald J. Trump (@realDonaldTrump), Twitter (Dec. 18, 2020, 9:14 AM)
(http://www.trumptwitterarchive.com/archive)

Donald J. Trump (@realDonaldTrump), Twitter (Dec. 19, 2020, 1:42 AM)
(http://www.trumptwitterarchive.com/archive)

Donald J. Trump (@realDonaldTrump), Twitter (Dec. 30, 2020, 2:38 PM)
(http://www.trumptwitterarchive.com/archive)

Donald J. Trump (@realDonaldTrump) (Jan. 1, 2021, 2:23 PM)
(http://www.trumptwitterarchive.com/archive)

Donald J. Trump (@realDonaldTrump), Twitter (Jan. 3, 2021, 10:27 AM)
(http://www.trumptwitterarchive.com/archive)

Donald J. Trump (@realDonaldTrump), Twitter (Jan. 5, 2021, 5:05 PM)
(http://www.trumptwitterarchive.com/archive)

Donald J. Trump (@realDonaldTrump), Twitter (Jan. 5, 2021, 5:12 PM)
(http://www.trumptwitterarchive.com/archive)

Donald J. Trump (@realDonaldTrump), Twitter (Jan. 6, 2021, 12:08 AM)
(http://www.trumptwitterarchive.com/archive)

Donald J. Trump (@realDonaldTrump), Twitter (Jan. 6, 2021, 12:16:00 AM)
(http://www.trumptwitterarchive.com/archive)

Donald J. Trump (@realDonaldTrump), Twitter (Jan. 6, 2021, 12:16:10 AM) (http://www.trumptwitterarchive.com/archive)

Donald J. Trump (@realDonaldTrump), Twitter (Jan. 6, 2021, 12:17:43 AM) (http://www.trumptwitterarchive.com/archive)

Donald J. Trump (@realDonaldTrump), Twitter (Jan. 6, 2021, 12:17:52 AM) (http://www.trumptwitterarchive.com/archive)

Donald J. Trump (@realDonaldTrump), Twitter (Jan. 6, 2021, 12:43 AM) (http://www.trumptwitterarchive.com/archive)

Donald J. Trump (@realDonaldTrump), Twitter (Jan. 6, 2021, 12:46 AM) (http://www.trumptwitterarchive.com/archive)

Donald J. Trump (@realDonaldTrump), Twitter (Jan. 6, 2021, 12:47 AM) (http://www.trumptwitterarchive.com/archive)

Donald J. Trump (@realDonaldTrump), Twitter (Jan. 6, 2021, 1:00 AM) (http://www.trumptwitterarchive.com/archive)

Donald J. Trump (@realDonaldTrump), Twitter (Jan. 6, 2021, 8:06 AM) (http://www.trumptwitterarchive.com/archive)

Donald J. Trump (@realDonaldTrump), Twitter (Jan. 6, 2021, 8:17 AM) (http://www.trumptwitterarchive.com/archive)

Donald J. Trump (@realDonaldTrump), Twitter (Jan. 6, 2021, 8:22 AM) (http://www.trumptwitterarchive.com/archive)

Donald J. Trump (@realDonaldTrump), Twitter (Jan. 6, 2021, 1:49 PM) (http://www.trumptwitterarchive.com/archive)

Donald J. Trump (@realDonaldTrump), Twitter (Jan. 6, 2021, 2:24 PM) (http://www.trumptwitterarchive.com/archive)

Donald J. Trump (@realDonaldTrump), Twitter (Jan. 6, 2021, 2:38 PM) (http://www.trumptwitterarchive.com/archive)

Donald J. Trump (@realDonaldTrump), Twitter (Jan. 6, 2021, 4:17 PM) (http://www.trumptwitterarchive.com/archive)

Donald J. Trump (@realDonaldTrump), Twitter (Jan. 6, 2021, 6:01 PM) (http://www.trumptwitterarchive.com/archive)

Donald J. Trump (@realDonaldTrump), Twitter (Jan. 7, 2021, 7:10 PM) (http://www.trumptwitterarchive.com/archive)

Donald J. Trump (@realDonaldTrump), Twitter (Jan. 8, 2021, 9:46 AM) (http://www.trumptwitterarchive.com/archive)

Donald J. Trump (@realDonaldTrump), Twitter (Jan. 8, 2021, 10:44 AM) (http://www.trumptwitterarchive.com/archive)

Dorf on Law (@dorfonlaw), Twitter (Jan. 6, 2021, 3:10 PM) (https://twitter.com/dorfonlaw/status/1346911948546269184)

H.R. McMaster (@LTGHRMcMaster), Twitter (Jan. 7, 2021, 3:05 PM) (https://twitter.com/LTGHRMcMaster/status/1347273185641734144)

Igor Bobic (@igorbobic), Twitter (Jan. 6, 2021, 2:02 PM) (https://twitter.com/igorbobic/status/1346895006263631872?s=20)

Igor Bobic (@igorbobic), Twitter (Jan. 6, 2021, 2:05 PM) (https://twitter.com/igorbobic/status/1346895569277628417)

Igor Bobic (@igorbobic), Twitter (Jan . 6, 2021, 2:16 PM) (https://twitter.com/igorbobic/status/1346898433689399297)

Igor Bobic (@igorbobic), Twitter (Jan . 6, 2021, 2:20 PM) (https://twitter.com/igorbobic/status/1346899437520621568)

Igor Bobic (@igorbobic), Twitter (Jan . 6, 2021, 2:24 PM) (https://twitter.com/igorbobic/status/1346900359353163779)

Igor Bobic (@igorbobic), Twitter (Jan . 6, 2021, 2:31 PM) (https://twitter.com/igorbobic/status/1346902299466203145)

Igor Bobic (@igorbobic), Twitter (Jan . 6, 2021, 2:45 PM) (https://twitter.com/igorbobic/status/1346905872157577222)

Igor Bobic (@igorbobic), Twitter (Jan. 6, 2021 2:47 PM) (https://twitter.com/igorbobic/status/1346906369232920576)

Igor Bobic (@igorbobic), Twitter (Jan . 6, 2021, 2:57 PM) (https://twitter.com/igorbobic/status/1346908735059456005)

Igor Bobic (@igorbobic), Twitter (Jan . 6, 2021, 3:09 PM) (https://twitter.com/igorbobic/status/1346911809274478594)

Jordan Novet (@jordannovet), Twitter (Jan. 7, 2021, 12:49 PM) (https://twitter.com/jordannovet/status/1347239013711818754)

Jordan Novet (@jordannovet), Twitter (Jan. 7, 2021, 12:50 PM) (https://twitter.com/jordannovet/status/1347239272189992965)

Kaitlan Collins (@kaitlancollins), Twitter (Jan. 6, 2021, 10:34 PM) (https://twitter.com/kaitlancollins/status/1347023890959228933)

Kayleigh McEnany (@PressSec), Twitter (Jan. 6, 2021, 3:36 PM) (https://twitter.com/PressSec/status/1346918582832168964)

Maggie Haberman (@maggieNYT), Twitter (Jan. 6, 2021, 11:19 PM) (https://twitter.com/mknz/status/1347036422360813571)

Mick Mulvaney (@MickMulvaney), Twitter (Jan. 6, 2021, 3:01 PM) (https://twitter.com/MickMulvaney/status/1346909665423196162)

Mike Pence (@Mike_Pence), Twitter (Jan. 6, 2021, 1:02 PM) (https://twitter.com/Mike_Pence/status/1346879811151605762?s=20)

President of Zimbabwe (@edmnangagwa), Twitter (Jan. 7, 2021, 8:42 AM) (https://twitter.com/edmnangagwa/status/1347176848694931457)

Rep. Dan Killdee (@RepDanKildee), Twitter (Jan. 6, 2021, 2:52 PM) (https://twitter.com/RepDanKildee/status/1346907565482004495)

Rep. Elaine Luria (@RepElaineLuria), Twitter (Jan. 6, 2021, 1:46 PM) (https://twitter.com/RepElaineLuria/status/1346890833266683904)

Rep. Sean Patrick Maloney (@RepSeanMaloney), Twitter (Jan. 8, 2021 2:28 PM) (https://twitter.com/repseanmaloney/status/1347626297367941121?s=27)

Senator Jeff Merkley (@SenJeffMerkley), Twitter (Jan. 6, 2021, 11:36 PM) (https://twitter.com/SenJeffMerkley/status/1347039504528498688)

Tom Williams (@pennstatetom), Twitter (Jan. 6, 2021, 4:30 PM) (https://twitter.com/pennstatetom/status/1346932134389313536)

Twitter Safety (@TwitterSafety), Twitter (Jan. 8, 2021, 6:21 PM) (https://twitter.com/TwitterSafety/status/1347684877634838528)

Zak Hudak (@cbszak), Twitter (Jan. 6, 2021, 4:01 PM) (https://twitter.com/cbszak/status/1346924751546175492

Photos and Videos

Are we allowed access to Capitol Hill offices and chambers on Jan. 6?, THE DONALD, (last visited Jan. 10, 2021) (https://thedonald.win/p/11RNfLzAy0/are-we-allowed-access-to-capitol/c/)

Chris Christie says Trump should tell protesters to leave Capitol, ABC NEWS (Jan. 6, 2021) (https://abcnews.go.com/US/video/chris-christie-trump-protesters-leave-capitol-75093817)

Derrick Evans, West Virginia lawmaker, filmed during US Capitol riot, Guardian News (Jan. 8, 2021) (https://www.youtube.com/watch?v=4dKyreFllgQ)

Donald Trump Vlog: Contesting Election Results - December 22, 2020 (Dec. 22, 2020) (https://www.youtube.com/watch?v=YJ8LfWC1Wks&feature=emb_logo)

Gabriel Sterling of Sec of State's Office Blasts Those Threatening Election Workers, GPB (Dec. 1, 2020) (https://www.youtube.com/watch?v=jLi-Yo6IucQ.1, 2020)

Hear photographer describe terrifying moment on Capitol Hill, CNN (Jan. 9, 2021) (https://www.cnn.com/videos/us/2021/01/10/officer-crushed-capitol-riot-video-jon-farina-sot-vpx.cnn)

John Kelly says he would vote to invoke 25th Amendment, CNN (Jan. 6, 2021) (https://www.youtube.com/watch?v=8UzqChhaTP8)

Lawmaker describes moment captured in dramatic photo, CNN (Jan. 6, 2021) (https://www.youtube.com/watch?v=cufftGM8040)

No surrender. No concession. The Capitol Building belongs to us if they don't fix the November mess, The Donald (https://thedonald.win/p/11RNy0wFCb/no-surrender-no-concession-the-c/)

Officer crushed in door by rioters at US Capitol, CNN (Jan. 9, 2021) (https://www.cnn.com/videos/us/2021/01/09/officer-crushed-in-door-capitol-riots-lemon-reaction-ctn-vpx.cnn)

'Proud Boys, stand back and stand by': Trump doesn't condemn white supremacists at debate, Wash. Post (Sep. 29, 2020) (https://www.washingtonpost.com/video/politics/proud-boys-stand-back-and-stand-by-trump-doesnt-condemn-white-supremacists-at-debate/2020/09/29/7b22d025-ce73-4f38-879e-d3740b9c1339_video.html)

Rep. Kildee Discusses Insurrection at U.S. Capitol During Electoral College Vote Certification, Congressman Dan Kildee (Jan. 7, 2021) (https://www.youtube.com/watch?v=AKYdyTYz6Jw)

See stunning video of rioters inside Capitol, CNN (Jan. 6, 2021) (https://www.youtube.com/watch?v=y9WPuA6EUaw)

Speech: Donald Trump Holds a Political Rally in Dalton, Georgia - January 4, 2021 (Jan. 4, 2021) (https://www.youtube.com/watch?v=kL_IpqRf8RM)

Speech: Donald Trump Holds a Political Rally in Valdosta, Georgia - December 5, 2020 (Dec. 5, 2020) (https://www.youtube.com/watch?v=hKBZemnS1j4&feature=emb_logo)

Speech: Donald Trump Holds a Political Rally on The Ellipse - January 6, 2021 (Jan. 6, 2021) (https://www.youtube.com/watch?v=RTK1lm1jk60&feature=emb_logo)

The capitol is our goal. Everything else is a distraction. Every corrupt member of congress locked in one room and surrounded by real Americans is an opportunity that will never present itself again, THE DONALD, (last visited Jan. 10, 2021) (https://thedonald.win/p/11ROLcUa9Y/the-capitol-is-our-goal--everyth/c/)

This many patriots would storm the capitol if President Trump orders it on January 6th., THE DONALD, (last visited Jan. 10, 2021) (https://thedonald.win/p/11ROLVhJcx/this-many-patriots-would-storm-t/)

Trump Supporters Threaten to Hang Mike Pence at Capitol (Jan. 8, 2021) (https://www.youtube.com/watch?v=Fag0aC_M0_U)

Watch a timeline of the U.S. Capitol siege that rocked America, CNBC Television (Jan. 7, 2021) (https://www.youtube.com/watch?v=DOemCrZac4M)

Watch LIVE: Save America March at The Ellipse featuring President @realDonaldTrump, RSBN TV (Jan. 6, 2020) (https://www.pscp.tv/w/1eaJbnwgERXJX?t=3h32m2s)

Congressional Documents

165 Cong. Rec. H12130-H12206 (daily ed. December 18, 2019)
(https://www.congress.gov/116/crec/2019/12/18/CREC-2019-12-18-pt1-PgH12130.pdf)

Constitution, Jefferson's Manual, Rules of the House of Representatives of the United States, H.
Doc. No. 115-177 § 603 (2019 ed.) (https://www.govinfo.gov/content/pkg/HMAN-
116/pdf/HMAN-116-jeffersonman.pdf)

Electoral Count Act of 1887, Pub. L. 49-90, 24 Stat. 373
(https://govtrackus.s3.amazonaws.com/legislink/pdf/stat/24/STATUTE-24-Pg373.pdf)

H. Doc. 116-95 (https://www.govinfo.gov/app/details/CDOC-116hdoc95/context)

H. Mis. Doc. No. 42, 40th Cong. (1868)
(https://www.senate.gov/artandhistory/history/common/briefing/Impeachment_Johnson.htm#7)

H. Rept. 116-346 (https://www.congress.gov/116/crpt/hrpt346/CRPT-116hrpt346.pdf)

H. Res.755, 116th Cong. (https://www.congress.gov/116/bills/hres755/BILLS-116hres755ih.pdf)
(2019)

Papers of John Adams vol. 2 p. 314, Massachusetts Historical Society
(http://www.masshist.org/publications/adams-papers/index.php/view/PJA02p314)

Staff of H. Comm. on the Judiciary, 116th Cong. Constitutional Grounds for Presidential
Impeachment (Comm. Print 2019) (https://www.govinfo.gov/content/pkg/CPRT-
116HPRT38513/pdf/CPRT-116HPRT38513.pdf)

S. Doc 116-12 (https://www.govinfo.gov/content/pkg/CDOC-116sdoc12/pdf/CDOC-116sdoc12-
pt1.pdf) (https://www.govinfo.gov/content/pkg/CDOC-116sdoc12/pdf/CDOC-116sdoc12-
pt2.pdf) (https://www.govinfo.gov/content/pkg/CDOC-116sdoc12/pdf/CDOC-116sdoc12-
pt3.pdf)

THE CONSTITUTION OF THE UNITED STATES

We the people of the United States, in Order to form a more perfect Union, establish Justice, insure domestic Tranquility, provide for the common defense, promote the general Welfare, and secure the Blessings of Liberty to ourselves and our Posterity, do ordain and establish this Constitution for the United States of America.

ARTICLE I

Section 1. All legislative Powers herein granted shall be vested in a Congress of the United States, which shall consist of a Senate and House of Representatives.

Section 2. The House of Representatives shall be composed of Members chosen every second Year by the People of the several States, and the Electors in each State shall have the Qualifications requisite for Electors of the most numerous Branch of the State Legislature. No Person shall be a Representative who shall not have attained to the Age of twenty five Years, and been seven Years a citizen of the United States, and who shall not, when elected, be an Inhabitant of that State in which he shall be chosen.

[Representatives and direct Taxes shall be apportioned among the several States which may be included within this Union, according to their respective Numbers, which shall be determined by adding to the whole Number of free Persons, including those bound to Service for a Term of Years, and excluding Indians not taxed, three fifths of all other Persons.][1] The actual Enumeration shall be made within three Years after the first Meeting of the Congress of the United States, and within every subsequent Term of ten Years, in such Manner as they shall by Law direct. The number of Representatives shall not exceed one for every thirty Thousand, but each State shall have at Least one Representative; and until such enumeration shall be made, the State of New Hampshire shall be entitled to chuse three, Massachusetts eight, Rhode-Island and Providence Plantations one, Connecticut five, New-York six, New Jersey four, Pennsylvania eight, Delaware one, Maryland six, Virginia ten, North Carolina five, South Carolina five, and Georgia three.

When vacancies happen in the Representation from any State, the Executive Authority thereof shall issue Writs of Election to fill such Vacancies.

The House of Representatives shall chuse their Speaker and other Officers; and shall have the sole Power of Impeachment.

1: *Changed by section 2 of the Fourteenth Amendment.*

Section 3. The Senate of the United States shall be composed of two Senators from each State, [chosen by the legislature thereof,]² for six Years; and each Senator shall have one Vote. Immediately after they shall be assembled in Consequence of the first Election, they shall be divided as equally as may be into three Classes. The Seats of the Senators of the first Class shall be vacated at the Expiration of the second Year, of the second Class at the Expiration of the fourth Year, and of the third Class at the expiration of the sixth Year, so that one third may be chosen every second Year; [and if vacancies happen by Resignation, or otherwise, during the Recess of the Legislature of any State, the Executive thereof may make temporary Appointments until the next Meeting of the Legislature, which shall then fill such Vacancies.]³

No person shall be a Senator who shall not have attained to the Age of thirty Years, and been nine Years a Citizen of the United States, and who shall not, when elected, be an Inhabitant of that State for which he shall be chosen.

The Vice President of the United States shall be President of the Senate, but shall have no Vote, unless they be equally divided.

The Senate shall chuse their other Officers, and also a President pro tempore, in the Absence of the Vice-President, or when he shall exercise the Office of President of the United States.

The Senate shall have the sole Power to try all Impeachments. When sitting for that Purpose, they shall be on Oath or Affirmation. When the President of the United States is tried,

2: *Changed by the Seventeenth Amendment.*
3: *Changed by the Seventeenth Amendment.*

the Chief Justice shall preside: And no Person shall be convicted without the Concurrence of two thirds of the Members present.

Judgment in Cases of Impeachment shall not extend further than to removal from Office, and disqualification to hold and enjoy any Office of honor, Trust or Profit under the United States: but the Party convicted shall nevertheless be liable and subject to Indictment, Trial, Judgment and Punishment, according to Law.

Section 4. The Times, Places and Manner of holding Elections for Senators and Representatives, shall be prescribed in each State by the Legislature thereof; but the Congress may at any time by Law make or alter such Regulations, except as to the Places of chusing Senators.

The Congress shall assemble at least once in every Year, and such Meeting shall be [on the first Monday in December,][4] unless they shall by law appoint a different Day.

Section 5. Each House shall be the Judge of the Elections, Returns and Qualifications of its own Members, and a Majority of each shall constitute a Quorum to do Business; but a smaller Number may adjourn from day to day, and may be authorized to compel the Attendance of absent Members, in such Manner, and under such Penalties as each House may provide.

Each house may determine the Rules of its Proceedings, punish its Members for disorderly Behavior, and, with the Concurrence of two-thirds, expel a Member.

4: *Changed by section 2 of the Twentieth Amendment.*

Each house shall keep a Journal of its Proceedings, and from time to time publish the same, excepting such Parts as may in their Judgment require Secrecy; and the Yeas and Nays of the Members of either House on any question shall, at the Desire of one fifth of those Present, be entered on the Journal.

Neither House, during the Session of Congress, shall, without the Consent of the other, adjourn for more than three days, nor to any other Place than that in which the two Houses shall be sitting.

Section 6. The Senators and Representatives shall receive a Compensation for their Services, to be ascertained by Law, and paid out of the Treasury of the United States. They shall in all Cases, except Treason, Felony and Breach of the Peace, be privileged from Arrest during their Attendance at the Session of their respective Houses, and in going to and returning from the same; and for any Speech or Debate in either House, they shall not be questioned in any other Place.

No Senator or Representative shall, during the Time for which he was elected, be appointed to any civil Office under the Authority of the United States, which shall have been created, or the Emoluments whereof shall have been encreased during such time; and no Person holding any Office under the United States, shall be a Member of either House during his Continuance in Office.

Section 7. All Bills for raising Revenue shall originate in the House of Representatives; but the Senate may propose or concur with Amendments as on other Bills.

Every Bill which shall have passed the House of Representatives and the Senate, shall, before it become a Law, be presented to the President of the United States; If he approve he shall sign it, but if not he shall return it, with his Objections to that House in which it shall have originated, who shall enter the Objections at large on their Journal, and proceed to reconsider it. If after such Reconsideration two thirds of that house shall agree to pass the Bill, it shall be sent, together with the Objections, to the other House, by which it shall likewise be reconsidered, and if approved by two thirds of that House, it shall become a Law. But in all such Cases the Votes of both Houses shall be determined by yeas and Nays, and the Names of the Persons voting for and against the Bill shall be entered on the Journal of each House respectively. If any Bill shall not be returned by the President within ten Days (Sundays excepted) after it shall have been presented to him, the Same shall be a Law, in like Manner as if he had signed it, unless the Congress by their Adjournment prevent its Return, in which case it shall not be a Law.

Every Order, Resolution, or Vote to which the Concurrence of the Senate and House of Representatives may be necessary (except on a question of Adjournment) shall be presented to the President of the United States; and before the Same shall take Effect, shall be approved by him, or being disapproved by him, shall be repassed by two thirds of the Senate and House of Representatives, according to the Rules and Limitations prescribed in the Case of a Bill.

Section 8. The Congress shall have Power To lay and collect Taxes, Duties, Imposts and Excises, to pay the Debts and provide for the common Defence and general Welfare of the United States; but all Duties, Imposts and Excises shall be uniform throughout the United States;

To borrow Money on the credit of the United States;

To regulate Commerce with foreign Nations, and among the several States, and with the Indian Tribes;

To establish an uniform Rule of Naturalization, and uniform Laws on the subject of Bankruptcies throughout the United States;

To coin Money, regulate the Value thereof, and of foreign Coin, and fix the Standard of Weights and Measures;

To provide for the Punishment of counterfeiting the Securities and current Coin of the United States;

To establish Post Offices and Post Roads;

To promote the Progress of Science and useful Arts, by securing for limited Times to Authors and Inventors the exclusive Right to their respective Writings and Discoveries;

To constitute Tribunals inferior to the supreme Court;

To define and punish Piracies and Felonies committed on the high Seas, and Offenses against the Law of Nations;

To declare War, grant Letters of Marque and Reprisal, and make Rules concerning Captures on Land and Water;

To raise and support Armies, but no Appropriation of Money to that Use shall be for a longer Term than two Years;

To provide and maintain a Navy;

To make Rules for the Government and Regulation of the land and naval Forces;

To provide for calling forth the Militia to execute the Laws of the Union, suppress Insurrections and repel Invasions;

To provide for organizing, arming, and disciplining, the Militia, and for governing such Part of them as may be employed in the Service of the United States, reserving to the States respectively, the Appointment of the Officers, and the Authority of training the Militia according to the discipline prescribed by Congress;

To exercise exclusive Legislation in all Cases whatsoever, over such District (not exceeding ten Miles square) as may, by Cession of particular States, and the Acceptance of Congress, become the Seat of the Government of the United States, and to exercise like Authority over all Places purchased by the Consent of the Legislature of the State in which the Same shall be, for the Erection of Forts, Magazines, Arsenals, dock-Yards, and other needful Buildings;—And

To make all Laws which shall be necessary and proper for carrying into Execution the foregoing Powers, and all other Powers vested by this Constitution in the Government of the United States, or in any Department or Officer thereof.

Section 9. The Migration or Importation of such Persons as any of the States now existing shall think proper to admit, shall not be prohibited by the Congress prior to the Year one thousand eight hundred and eight, but a Tax or Duty may be imposed on such Importation, not exceeding ten dollars for each Person.

The Privilege of the Writ of Habeas Corpus shall not be suspended, unless when in Cases of Rebellion or Invasion the public Safety may require it.

No Bill of Attainder or ex post facto Law shall be passed.

No Capitation, or other direct, Tax shall be laid, unless in Proportion to the Census or Enumeration herein before directed to be taken.[5]

No Tax or Duty shall be laid on Articles exported from any State.

No Preference shall be given by any Regulation of Commerce or Revenue to the Ports of one State over those of another: nor shall Vessels bound to, or from, one State, be obliged to enter, clear, or pay Duties in another.

No Money shall be drawn from the Treasury, but in Consequence of Appropriations made by Law; and a regular Statement and Account of the Receipts and Expenditures of all public Money shall be published from time to time.

No Title of Nobility shall be granted by the United States: And no Person holding any Office of Profit or Trust under them, shall, without the Consent of the Congress, accept of any present, Emolument, Office, or Title, of any kind whatever, from any King, Prince, or foreign State.

Section 10. No State shall enter into any Treaty, Alliance, or Confederation; grant Letters of Marque and Reprisal; coin Money; emit Bills of Credit; make any Thing but gold and silver Coin a Tender in Payment of Debts; pass any Bill of Attainder, ex post facto Law, or Law impairing the Obligation of Contracts, or grant any Title of Nobility.

No State shall, without the Consent of the Congress, lay any Imposts or Duties on Imports or Exports, except what may be absolutely necessary for executing it's inspection Laws: and the net Produce of all Duties and Imposts, laid by any State on

5: *See Sixteenth Amendment.*

Imports or Exports, shall be for the Use of the Treasury of the United States; and all such Laws shall be subject to the Revision and Controul of the Congress.

No State shall, without the Consent of Congress, lay any Duty of Tonnage, keep Troops, or Ships of War in time of Peace, enter into any Agreement or Compact with another State, or with a foreign Power, or engage in War, unless actually invaded, or in such imminent Danger as will not admit of delay.

ARTICLE II

Section 1. The executive Power shall be vested in a President of the United States of America. He shall hold his Office during the Term of four Years, and, together with the Vice President, chosen for the same Term, be elected, as follows:

Each State shall appoint, in such Manner as the Legislature thereof may direct, a Number of Electors, equal to the whole Number of Senators and Representatives to which the State may be entitled in the Congress: but no Senator or Representative, or Person holding an Office of Trust or Profit under the United States, shall be appointed an Elector.

[The Electors shall meet in their respective States, and vote by Ballot for two Persons, of whom one at least shall not be an Inhabitant of the same State with themselves. And they shall make a List of all the Persons voted for, and of the Number of Votes for each; which List they shall sign and certify, and transmit sealed to the Seat of the Government of the United States, directed to the President of the Senate. The President of the Senate shall, in the Presence of the Senate and House of Representatives, open all the Certificates, and the Votes shall then be counted. The Person having the greatest Number of Votes shall be the President, if such Number be a Majority of the whole Number of Electors appointed; and if there be more than one who have such Majority, and have an equal Number of Votes, then the House of Representatives shall immediately chuse by Ballot one of them for President; and if no Person have a Majority, then from the five highest on the List the said House shall in like Manner chuse the President. But in chusing the President, the Votes shall be taken by States, the Representation from each State having one Vote; a quorum for this Purpose shall consist of a Member or Members from two thirds of the States, and a Majority of all the States shall be necessary to a Choice. In every Case, after the Choice of the President, the Person having the greatest Number of Votes of the Electors shall be the Vice President. But if there should remain two or more who have equal Votes, the Senate shall chuse from them by Ballot the Vice President.][6]

The Congress may determine the Time of chusing the Electors, and the Day on which they shall give their Votes; which Day shall be the same throughout the United States.

No Person except a natural born Citizen, or a Citizen of the United States, at the time of the Adoption of this Constitution, shall be eligible to the Office of President; neither shall any person be eligible to that Office who shall not have attained to the Age of thirty five Years, and been fourteen Years a Resident within the United States.

6: *Changed by the Twenty-Fifth Amendment.*

[In Case of the Removal of the President from Office, or of his Death, Resignation, or Inability to discharge the Powers and Duties of the said Office, the Same shall devolve on the Vice President, and the Congress may by Law provide for the Case of Removal, Death, Resignation or Inability, both of the President and Vice President, declaring what Officer shall then act as President, and such Officer shall act accordingly, until the Disability be removed, or a President shall be elected.][7]

The President shall, at stated Times, receive for his Services, a Compensation, which shall neither be increased nor diminished during the Period for which he shall have been elected, and he shall not receive within that Period any other Emolument from the United States, or any of them.

Before he enter on the Execution of his Office, he shall take the following Oath or Affirmation:—"I do solemnly swear (or affirm) that I will faithfully execute the Office of President of the United States, and will to the best of my Ability, preserve, protect and defend the Constitution of the United States."

Section 2. The President shall be Commander in Chief of the Army and Navy of the United States, and of the Militia of the several States, when called into the actual Service of the United States; he may require the Opinion, in writing, of the principal Officer in each of the executive Departments, upon any Subject relating to the Duties of their respective Offices, and he shall have Power to grant Reprieves and Pardons for Offenses against the United States, except in Cases of impeachment.

7: *Changed by the Twenty-Fifth Amendment.*

He shall have Power, by and with the Advice and Consent of the Senate, to make Treaties, provided two thirds of the Senators present concur; and he shall nominate, and by and with the Advice and Consent of the Senate, shall appoint Ambassadors, other public Ministers and Consuls, Judges of the supreme Court, and all other Officers of the United States, whose Appointments are not herein otherwise provided for, and which shall be established by Law: but the Congress may by Law vest the Appointment of such inferior Officers, as they think proper, in the President alone, in the Courts of Law, or in the Heads of Departments.

The President shall have Power to fill up all Vacancies that may happen during the Recess of the Senate, by granting Commissions which shall expire at the End of their next session.

Section 3. He shall from time to time give to the Congress Information of the State of the Union, and recommend to their Consideration such Measures as he shall judge necessary and expedient; he may, on extraordinary Occasions, convene both Houses, or either of them, and in Case of Disagreement between them, with Respect to the Time of Adjournment, he may adjourn them to such Time as he shall think proper; he shall receive Ambassadors and other public Ministers; he shall take Care that the Laws be faithfully executed, and shall Commission all the Officers of the United States.

Section 4. The President, Vice President and all civil Officers of the United States, shall be removed from Office on Impeachment for, and Conviction of, Treason, Bribery, or other high Crimes and Misdemeanors.

ARTICLE III

Section 1. The judicial Power of the United States, shall be vested in one supreme Court, and in such inferior Courts as the Congress may from time to time ordain and establish. The Judges, both of the supreme and inferior Courts, shall hold their Offices during good Behaviour, and shall, at stated Times, receive for their Services, a Compensation, which shall not be diminished during their Continuance in Office.

Section 2. The judicial Power shall extend to all Cases, in Law and Equity, arising under this Constitution, the Laws of the United States, and Treaties made, or which shall be made, under their Authority;—to all Cases affecting Ambassadors, other public Ministers and Consuls;—to all Cases of admiralty and maritime Jurisdiction;—to Controversies to which the United States shall be a Party;—to Controversies between two or more States;—[between a State and Citizens of another State;—]⁸between Citizens of different States;—between Citizens of the same State claiming Lands under Grants of different States, and [between a State, or the Citizens thereof, and foreign States, Citizens or Subjects.]

In all cases affecting Ambassadors, other public Ministers and Consuls, and those in which a State shall be Party, the supreme Court shall have original Jurisdiction. In all the other

8: *Changed by the Eleventh Amendment.*

Cases before mentioned, the supreme Court shall have appellate Jurisdiction, both as to Law and Fact, with such Exceptions, and under such Regulations as the Congress shall make.

The Trial of all Crimes, except in Cases of Impeachment, shall be by Jury; and such Trial shall be held in the State where the said Crimes shall have been committed; but when not committed within any State, the Trial shall be at such Place or Places as the Congress may by Law have directed.

Section 3. Treason against the United States, shall consist only in levying War against them, or in adhering to their Enemies, giving them Aid and Comfort. No Person shall be convicted of Treason unless on the Testimony of two Witnesses to the same overt Act, or on Confession in open Court.

The Congress shall have power to declare the punishment of Treason, but no Attainder of Treason shall work Corruption of Blood, or Forfeiture except during the Life of the Person attainted.

ARTICLE IV

Section 1. Full Faith and Credit shall be given in each State to the public Acts, Records, and judicial Proceedings of every other State; And the Congress may by general Laws prescribe the Manner in which such Acts, Records and Proceedings shall be proved, and the Effect thereof.

Section 2. The Citizens of each State shall be entitled to all Privileges and Immunities of Citizens in the several States.

A Person charged in any State with Treason, Felony, or other Crime, who shall flee from Justice, and be found in another State, shall on Demand of the executive Authority of the State from which he fled, be delivered up, to be removed to the State having Jurisdiction of the Crime.

[No person held to Service or Labour in one State, under the Laws thereof, escaping into another, shall, in Consequence of any Law or Regulation therein, be discharged from such Service or Labour, But shall be delivered up on Claim of the Party to whom such Service or Labor may be due.][9]

Section 3. New States may be admitted by the Congress into this Union; but no new States shall be formed or erected within the Jurisdiction of any other State; nor any State be formed by the Junction of two or more States, or Parts of States, without the Consent of the Legislatures of the States concerned as well as of the Congress.

The Congress shall have Power to dispose of and make all needful Rules and Regulations respecting the Territory or other Property belonging to the United States; and nothing in this Constitution shall be so construed as to Prejudice any Claims of the United States, or of any particular State.

Section 4. The United States shall guarantee to every State in this Union a Republican Form of Government, and shall protect each of them against Invasion; and on Application of the Legislature, or of the Executive (when the Legislature cannot be convened) against domestic Violence.

9: *Changed by the Thirteenth Amendment.*

ARTICLE V

The Congress, whenever two thirds of both Houses shall deem it necessary, shall propose Amendments to this Constitution, or, on the Application of the Legislatures of two thirds of the several States, shall call a Convention for proposing Amendments, which, in either Case, shall be valid to all Intents and Purposes, as Part of this Constitution, when ratified by the Legislatures of three fourths of the several States, or by Conventions in three fourths thereof, as the one or the other Mode of Ratification may be proposed by the Congress; Provided that no Amendment which may be made prior to the Year one thousand eight hundred and eight shall in any Manner affect the first and fourth Clauses in the ninth Section of the first Article; and that no State, without its Consent, shall be deprived of it's equal Suffrage in the Senate.

ARTICLE VI

All Debts contracted and Engagements entered into, before the Adoption of this Constitution, shall be as valid against the United States under this Constitution, as under the Confederation.

This Constitution, and the Laws of the United States which shall be made in Pursuance thereof; and all Treaties made, or which shall be made, under the Authority of the United States, shall be the supreme Law of the Land; and the Judges in every State shall be bound thereby, any Thing in the Constitution or Laws of any State to the Contrary notwithstanding.

The Senators and Representatives before mentioned, and the Members of the several State Legislatures, and all executive and judicial Officers, both of the United States and of the several

States, shall be bound by Oath or Affirmation, to support this Constitution; but no religious Test shall ever be required as a Qualification to any Office or public Trust under the United States

ARTICLE VII

The Ratification of the Conventions of nine States, shall be sufficient for the Establishment of this Constitution between the States so ratifying the Same.

done in Convention by the Unanimous Consent of the States present the Seventeenth Day of September in the Year of our Lord one thousand seven hundred and Eighty seven and of the Independence of the United States of America the Twelfth

In Witness whereof We have hereunto subscribed our Names,
Go. WASHINGTON
          Presid. and deputy from Virginia

New Hampshire
John Langdon
Nicholas Gilman
Massachusetts
Nathaniel Gorham
Rufus King
Connecticut
Wm. Saml. Johnson
Roger Sherman
New York
Alexander Hamilton

New Jersey
Will Livingston
David Brearley
Wm. Paterson
Jona: Dayton
Pennsylvania
B Franklin
Thomas Mifflin
Robt Morris
Geo: Clymer
Thos FitzSimons

Jared Ingersoll
James Wilson
Gouv Morris
Delaware
George Read
Gunning Bedford jun
John Dickinson
Richard Bassett
Jaco: Broom
Maryland
James Mchenry
Dan of St Thos. Jenifer
Danl Carroll
Virginia
John Blair
James Madison Jr.

North Carolina
Wm. Blount
Rich'd Dobbs Spaight
Hu Williamson
South Carolina
J. Rutledge
Charles Cotesworth Pinckney
Charles Pinckney
Pierce Butler
Georgia
William Few
Abr Baldwin

Attest:
William Jackson, Secretary